Teaching English Spelling

A practical guide

Ruth Shemesh and
Sheila Waller

Consultant and editor: Penny Ur

CAMBRIDGE
UNIVERSITY PRESS

CAMBRIDGE UNIVERSITY PRESS
Cambridge, New York, Melbourne, Madrid, Cape Town, Singapore, São Paulo, Delhi

Cambridge University Press
The Edinburgh Building, Cambridge CB2 8RU, UK

www.cambridge.org
Information on this title: www.cambridge.org/9780521639712

First published 2000
6th printing 2007

Printed in the United Kingdom at the University Press, Cambridge

A catalogue record for this publication is available from the British Library

ISBN 978-0-521-63971-2 paperback

Contents

Contents

Thanks

Our thanks to the pupils, colleagues, friends and especially K. S. at Hof HaCarmel School who helped us realize our dream, and to Penny Ur, our guide.

Introduction

Why we wrote this book

We started to write this book for two reasons: desperation and guilt. We were desperate because our middle school and high school students repeated their spelling mistakes year after year. We felt guilty because, as English teachers of non-native speakers, we had but few teaching remedies. When 'spelling' was discussed in the staff meetings, we would focus on such questions as: 'How much to correct?' and 'How many marks should be deducted for poor spelling?'

It seemed that both teachers and students had succumbed, unknowingly, to two 'nature–nurture' spelling myths: one saying that good spellers are born and not made; the other saying, give students enough reading and writing to do, and spelling will teach itself. If either of these statements were true for everyone, then why should we try to re-introduce spelling? One thing disturbed us: there seemed to be a fair number of students we considered 'good readers' whose written work had many spelling errors.

Having no answers, we returned to teaching our conventional repertoire of spelling patterns, most of them connected to grammar (for example, when to add '-s', '-es', or '-ies' when forming a plural). It wasn't until Ruth Shemesh, a fellow colleague (and one of the authors of this book) shared with us, in a staff meeting, what she had learned at a training course for the Hickey method of teaching English reading and writing skills to dyslexics that things began to change. The Hickey method (Hickey, 1977) like the Orton-Gillingham and Bangor methods, teaches spelling patterns using phonemes (units of sound) and graphemes (the letter or letters representing the phoneme). We knew that English teachers used a phonetically based system when teaching reading and writing skills to their students in elementary school. It had never occurred to us that we should review it in later grades.

It was a memorable staff meeting. For the first time, we saw that spelling was more than a few maxims, like *Magic 'E'*, and the rhyme, *I before E, except after C*. Ruth put together a pamphlet to help us all 'teach spelling'. Our students responded positively. They liked the idea of 'rules', even if their teachers called them 'spelling patterns'. (A 'rule' should be one hundred per cent true.) The students liked it even more when the teachers explained that if they heard a particular sound, a relevant spelling pattern (or a limited choice of spelling patterns) could represent it. Most teachers were enthusiastic, too – we were finally doing something. But, as it turned out, we weren't doing it very well. The spelling generalizations were unaccompanied by a detailed explanation, thus, some of us were confused! There were also no practice exercises for the students. No practice, no learning! Slowly, the teachers abandoned the new spelling programme, some more quickly than others – a fact many students didn't mind, since it had become a trifle boring.

The long list of spelling patterns was shelved, until the monotony of students' spelling errors forced us to ask, once again:

- *Why can't they spell?*
- *Which spelling patterns do we teach, and how do we organize them?*
- *What should the lesson plan include?*
- *What should be our criteria for the practice activities?*
- *What and how do we test?*

Our answers to these are explained more fully below.

Why can't they spell?

1 Blame history

English spelling and pronunciation seem full of 'inconsistencies'. We can probably thank history for that. From 400 BC to 1066 AD, there were many invasions that resulted in permanent settlements in various parts of Britain: the Celts; the Romans; early Christian missionaries educated in Latin and Greek; the Angles, Jutes and Saxons with their Germanic dialects (which formed the basis of today's English language); the Vikings; and finally, the Normans headed by King William, bringing French to England's court. Though the first English dictionary was eventually written in 1623, this did not mean there was a consensus on pronunciation – then, as today, geographical differences affected one's speech. Nor was there a consensus on spelling. An additional problem was created by gradual changes in the way people pronounced English: the sounds changed, but fewer written symbols for these sounds did. Today, several of these 'frozen' spelling patterns are, for students, pure enigmas, as for example is 'gh' in *cough*, *through* and *ghost*.

2 Blame the alphabet

One author has described English spelling as 'an awesome mess', 'irrational', and even 'inhuman' (Mario Pei, 1965). There are too many sounds for too few letters. The English alphabet consists of 26 letters used singly or in combinations to write the approximately 44 sounds in English speech. Sometimes, there is a direct relationship of letter to sound, as in the spelling of *man*. Other times, one sound may have as many as 14 different spellings, as does the sound 'sh' in *station*, *special*, and *charades*, to name but three. No wonder there are organizations whose aim is to simplify spelling! Unfortunately, their crusades have yet to effect a noticeable change and we must continue the struggle with learning to spell, but how? Learning to spell by using only the whole-word method requires an excellent visual memory. We are left with identifying sound-letter patterns, even if there are more than one for a particular sound. The 'awesome mess' can be reduced, but never banished.

3 Blame the number of language-processing skills one needs to spell accurately

Listed below are some of the language-processing skills one might need for accurate spelling:

- Be able to hear the sounds correctly.
- Be able to pronounce words correctly.
- Be able to remember all the word's phonemes in the correct order (some people might hear the word *capable* but remember it as *cabaple*).
- Be able to recognize the letters of the alphabet and know the sounds they represent.
- Be able to organize and remember the correct order of the letters in a word (*saw* might be written as *was*).
- Be able to copy words correctly from another source.
- Be able to discern between similar looking letters (*d–p–b–q, m–w, n–h, n–u, t–f*).
- Be able to learn new vocabulary, to use it and recognize it, since it is more difficult to spell unfamiliar words.
- Be able to understand and use affixes as well as to recognize their spelling patterns, for example, *de-, con-, re-, -ing, -ed, -er, -est*.

Sometimes, non-native English students need additional skills. They may have to learn a different letter and/or sound code. They also may have to learn a new language direction (as do students whose mother tongue is Arabic, Japanese, Hebrew or Chinese) in order to write and read from left to right, when their mother tongue may be right to left, or top to bottom.

For some students, learning to read and write is more difficult than it is for others. Possible reasons for their difficulties include dyslexia (in its many forms), attention deficiency problems and/or a short-term memory problem. Most students will experience some difficulties when learning to read and write in their mother tongue, but those with learning disorders will have far more.

Which spelling patterns do we teach? How do we organize them?

Our students' written work partially answered this question for us. Many of their spelling errors resulted from poor phoneme awareness, especially with vowel sounds, and a few consonant sounds. Other errors resulted from changes which occur at the end of some words when adding a suffix, as well as letter substitutions, especially when they represent the same or a similar sound, like 'c' for 'k' when hearing the sound /k/. Some students applied the same spelling pattern whenever a particular sound was heard, ignoring the existence of other patterns for the same sound. Obviously, we had to show them how to consider other spelling options.

In addition to our students' errors, we gained more insight by reading an overview of research on spelling errors (Scott, Foresman & Co., 1995) where vowel errors were cited as the leading cause for misspelled words, followed by consonant errors, and the adding of affixes. These findings at least explained what was happening with our students.

Finally, by studying other spelling manuals we tried to determine whether we were guilty of serious omissions. We could not possibly include all the spelling patterns in the English language, but we tried to include those which are frequently used and the cause of spelling errors.

In general, our guide for organizing the spelling patterns into units was based on finding patterns that had the same basic sound. When this was not possible, we classed together spelling patterns that followed a particular sound phenomenon, as found in Unit 3 (the spelling patterns all follow the short vowel sound) and Unit 9 (the letters 'c' and 'g' have two basic sounds: 'soft' and 'hard'). However, the first unit introduces students to long and short vowel sounds and their connection to syllables, since this information is often needed to understand the explanations to some of the spelling patterns. The final unit includes suffixes and silent letters, which do not share a common sound.

What should the lesson plan include?

In writing the lesson plans, we used suggestions made by other teachers as well as our own ideas. Essentially, what we wanted to provide were the following points:

- easy to follow instructions, with clearly defined stages.
- additional background information to the spelling pattern for the teacher to use, according to the needs of the class.
- heterogeneous tasks and quizzes that were appropriate for various ability levels.
- photocopiable exercises and activities.
- a repeatable framework for the lesson, to help with continuity, especially if spelling lessons were to be a 'once a week' event.
- student involvement.

In reference to the last point, the lesson plan tries to involve the students, not only when eliciting words for the board, but also by getting them to notice common factors affecting the spelling pattern. We have found that the spelling patterns become more meaningful (and memorable) this way. However, students need to be taught how to do this, and non-native speakers might feel more comfortable doing it in their mother tongue. Here is a short checklist of 'clues' to share with your students:

- ✓ Is a short or long vowel sound affecting the spelling pattern? (as in *pin–pine*)
- ✓ Is the spelling pattern found in single syllable or multi-syllable words? ('-ic' is rarely found in a single syllable word)
- ✓ Is the position of the new spelling pattern a factor to consider? ('-qu' never ends a word)
- ✓ Is the new spelling pattern repeatedly accompanied by a another letter? (The silent 'l' is usually followed by 'm' (*calm*), 'k' (*walk*), 'd' (*would*), and 'f' (*half*).

What should be our criteria for the practice activities?

Listening practice

Initially, we went straight into a written activity – since there were no 'warm-up, listening exercises' to do. This was not fair to our students. They first needed to strengthen their visual-auditory recognition (phoneme awareness) of the new spelling pattern before being asked to use it correctly in one of the written activities. The listening practice exercises in this book are like dictations, where varying demands are made, according to the class level. They allow students to self-check their understanding of both the sound and the spelling of the new pattern.

Meaningful learning

We wanted these exercises to be meaningful, giving students an opportunity to use the new spelling patterns in a significant manner. Our students' preference for word games as a significant medium for using language resulted in this book including many activities like trivia, wordsearches, crosswords, picture identifications and the like. Equally important for us was to involve the different language skills of reading, writing, listening and oral work. This we could do through exercises which asked the students to share information, such as in pair crossword puzzles. Additional bonuses, not planned for, were that many exercises contributed to the learning of some new vocabulary items, and sometimes, grammar.

Maintain motivation

In order to motivate continued learning, tasks could not be boring and repetitive, they had to be interesting enough for the student to *want* to complete them. Some are openly entertaining (as in competitions, drama, funny rhymes, stories). Finally, there are many open-ended activities which allow personal expression and creativity (make your own wordsearch, finish the story, draw a picture, make up rhyming headlines, etc.). A less obvious but important motivating factor is page layout. A variety of fonts and font sizes and the aesthetic positioning of text, graphic image, borders and banners affect all of us, even before we start to read the text.

Heterogeneity

No matter what kind of class we have, it is heterogeneous. Where mixed-level classes are the norm, heterogeneity increases. We tried to create exercises which were success-orientated, so as not to discourage learning, especially with less able students. Therefore, students are directed to 'do as many as you can', or 'do at least ...'. In addition, many lessons offer a choice of activities for each level. Some have alternative instructions, to allow for more teaching flexibility. Finally, at the end of each lesson are suggested test words at three proficiency levels.

What and how do we test?

From the beginning, it was important to build a record of the students' spelling achievements as the class progressed from pattern to pattern. Nevertheless, we did not want a student's fear of tests or quizzes to discourage or limit learning. When we explained that in the weekly quiz they would be tested on that week's spelling pattern *and* on preceding patterns, several students voiced their concern. However, after explaining that they would get a mark for correctly writing the 'spelling pattern', and another mark for correctly writing the whole word, the students were more relaxed. It is important to emphasize that students do *not* get a list of words from which to study for the quiz. This sometimes means a student may hear an unfamiliar word in the test, but he/she should be able to write it correctly by sounding out the letters and using the new spelling pattern(s). We have found that the weekly quiz, which takes less than five minutes, encourages students to review the weekly spelling pattern at home. Since their quiz results are usually high, they are quite proud of their achievements. Most quizzes are self-checked, then handed in to the teacher.

Some useful tips

We have found the following tips helpful in our teaching:

1 Teach one spelling pattern every week.
2 Spend 8–12 minutes introducing the spelling pattern, another five minutes doing the warm-up listening exercise, and as much time as your class needs to do and check the spelling activity.
3 If you teach non-native English students, try using the students' mother tongue, if possible, to introduce the spelling pattern and to write the 'rule' on the board.
4 You may want to have a 'spelling corner' to record/display the spelling patterns, as you teach them. Referring to previously taught patterns becomes easier this way.
5 Encourage your students to use a separate notebook or file for the weekly spelling patterns, example words and spelling activities.
6 Teach words listed as 'common exceptions' only if they are fairly important words that your class is likely to need.
7 Test the weekly spelling pattern a few days after teaching it. This shouldn't take long, and it can be a five-minute activity for the beginning or end of a lesson.
8 To reduce student tension, as well as your own teaching load, try letting the students grade their own spelling quiz, by comparing their answers to those you write up on the board. Occasionally,

you may want to check them yourself. We suggest that one mark be given for writing the correct spelling pattern, and another mark for spelling the whole word correctly.

9 You might like to encourage each student to record his/her spelling quizzes in a table or graph form, with the name of the spelling patterns as headings. For example:

SPELLING SCORE CARD (here, maximum 20)

	2	4	6	8	10	12	14	16	18	20
'C' or 'K'										
-'K' or '-CK'										

10 If, at the same time, other classes are learning the spelling patterns, you can suggest an inter-class spelling-bee every few months.

1 Vowel sounds

1.1 Short vowel sounds

Lesson plan

This unit deals with the students' listening awareness of both short and long vowel sounds. You might note that there is no universally agreed concept of what each vowel sound should be. Although this book uses the phonetic symbols from the International Phonetic Alphabet, which is based on Southern British English pronunciation, there are many other acceptable pronunciations which you could check in a good dictionary.

Each word, when sounded out, has one or more beats. Each beat is a syllable. In every beat (syllable) we usually hear a vowel sound. A vowel sound occurs when the mouth is open, the air can flow freely and the tongue is at rest. The vowels are 'a' 'e' 'i' 'o' 'u' and sometimes 'y'. One or two vowel letters may combine to make one sound, as you can see in the following:

one-syllable words	two-syllable words	three-syllable words
can	can - dy	can - di - date
hope	hope - ful	un - hope - ful
weight	weight - less	weight - less - ness

When writing, students may rely only on their auditory memory, that is, they write the way they remember the sound of a word. (The word 'week' may be written as 'wik', if that is what the students hear.) Therefore, in this unit, the differences between the various short vowel sounds are practised. Next, students are introduced to the differences between the short **and** long vowel sounds. Later units will deal with each long vowel sound individually.

1 ELICIT: Ask students for the names of the vowels. Write them on the board: A E I O U. Remind the students that all the other letters are called consonants, apart from **Y**, which sometimes acts as a vowel and other times as a consonant. (In less advanced bilingual classes, this part of the lesson can be done in mother tongue.)

2 WRITE ON THE BOARD:

a	e	i	o	u
cat	bed	big	hot	fun

Ask students to give other words that follow the same CVC (consonant – vowel – consonant) pattern of letters and add them to the table.

Students copy the table and three examples for each vowel into their notebooks.

3 ASK: What sound does each vowel have when it is 'sandwiched' between two consonants? Answer: The vowel does not say its name, but is pronounced as a short sound: /æ/ as in *cat*; /e/ as in *bed*; /ɪ/ as in *sit* ; /ɒ/ as in *hot* and /ʌ/ as in *fun*.

The vowel will be pronounced in its short form in VC words, like *at, it, up, on*.

You might want to explain to more advanced classes that this pronunciation does not apply to some one-syllable words that end in '-ld', '-st', or '-nd', where the vowel sound is long: /aɪ/ as in *kind, mind, child*; /əʊ/ as in *old, most, post*.

Warm-up practice of short vowel sounds

* *Beginners*
In turn, students say aloud to the rest of the class one short vowel sound, without revealing the name of the vowel being pronounced, for example, Student A says '/ɪ/' as in *sit*. The other students must guess which vowel is being referred to. Do this until all the vowel sounds have been covered and students feel confident in identifying the short vowel sounds.

* *Intermediate*
Write on the board:

bag   beg   big   bog   bug

You should now carefully pronounce each word out loud to the class. Tell the class that when the next word is called out, they must identify which word was said and write it down in their notebooks. It's a good idea to go over the correct answer after each word and possibly re-test words that were problematic for the students.

* *Advanced*
The following are a number of listening exercises that use the same list
of words and are aimed at strengthening the students' perception of
the five short vowel sounds. You could either write the list on the
board or photocopy it and hand out to each student.

Listening Exercise – Short Vowel Sounds

 1 bad   bed
 2 cop   cup
 3 bit   bat
 4 mud   mad
 5 chip chap chop
 6 drunk drink drank
 7 an   in   on
 8 pet   pit   pat
 9 hut   hot   hit   hat
10 bug   bag   big   beg

© Cambridge University Press 2000

1 Dictate one word from each line. Ask the students to underline the
  word they hear.

2 Another way you might like to consider is to read out all the words
  from each line, but at random. Students number the words in the
  order they hear them. For example, (line 5), the words are read out
  in the order of **chop**, **chip** and **chap**. The students would write their
  answer like this:

  2   3   1
  chip   chap   chop

3 Students work in pairs, taking turns reading out one word from
  each line. The partner must identify the word by pointing to it on
  the page.

4 Taking turns, one student dictates a word and the partner writes it
  down, without looking at the list.
    You might like to ask the students:

  • What difficulties did you have when doing these exercises?
  • What was easier for you?
  • Which sound/letter did you have most difficulty with?

A Beginners

1 What am I?

Circle the word that is the name of the picture. Do at least six.

cat cot cut **1**	bag big bug **2**	bad bud bed **3**
pin pan pen **4**	bit bat but **5**	hot hat hut **6**
cup cap cop **7**	dig dog dug **8**	track trick truck **9**

2 Pick a letter – make a word

Choose one letter from each box to make up the name of the picture. Write the name on the space at the side. Do at least seven.

1	b / r	a / e	m / d		_ _ _
2	d / b	o / u	k / x		_ _ _
3	f / p	i / a	t / n		_ _ _
4	p / d	e / o	g / q		_ _ _
5	t / k	i / e	n / d		_ _ _
6	r / b	a / u	s / c		_ _ _
7	z / s	o / u	n / b		_ _ _
8	sh / ch	e / i	p / f		_ _ _ _
9	pr / fr	a / o	g / j		_ _ _ _
10	f / d	u / i	nd / sh		_ _ _ _

3 Vowel trivia

Read the definition, then choose a suitable vowel to complete the word, which matches the definition. Can you do at least 14?

A   E   I   O   U

1 p __ g	a farm animal	11 d __ ck	a swimming bird
2 m __ p	found in an atlas	12 h __ t	not cold
3 r __ d	a colour	13 s __ x	a number
4 h __ nd	has fingers	14 w __ t	not dry
5 m __ n	not a woman	15 n __ ck	a giraffe's is long
6 l __ ps	part of the mouth	16 b __ d	not good
7 f __ x	a wild animal	17 dr __ ss	a girl may wear it
8 t __ n	a number	18 c __ p	you drink from it
9 g __ lf	a game	19 d __ sc	for the computer
10 r __ n	not walk	20 d __ ll	a child's toy

B Intermediate

1 Triangular words

In each triangle, write a three-letter word that is an answer to its clue. Write each letter of the word in the corners of the triangle. Make sure the word is written in the triangle with the same number as its clue. Words can be written either clockwise or counterclockwise. Where the corners of the triangles meet, the letters are the same. To help you start, the answer is given for clue five. Solve at least 15.

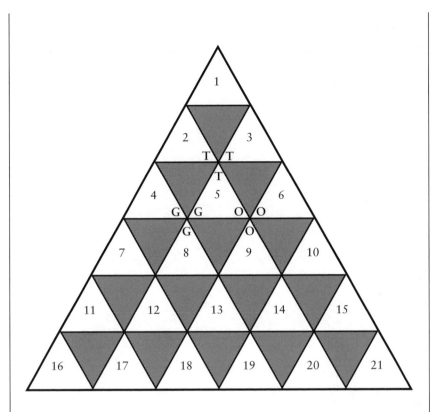

Clues

1 Not a woman
2 10
3 Turn it on for water
4 Precious stone
5 Received
6 Policeman
7 Earth and water
8 It covers the floor
9 To go bad
10 A lion, for example

11 Past of 'do'
12 It becomes a flower
13 One of many bones
14 A can
15 It blows air
16 To tear
17 A colour
18 Place to sleep in
19 Quickly in and out of water
20 Used for frying
21 Not thin

2 Compound word picturegram

In this exercise, there are picture, word and letter hints. Use them all and discover the compound words. Try to do at least ten.

1 + set   = _ _ _ _ _ _

2 + mill   = _ _ _ _ _ _ _ _

3 + stick   = _ _ _ _ _ _ _ _ _

4 + club   = _ _ _ _ _ _ _

5 + stick   = _ _ _ _ _ _ _ _

6 + = _ nth _ ll

7 + = s _ ndb _ x

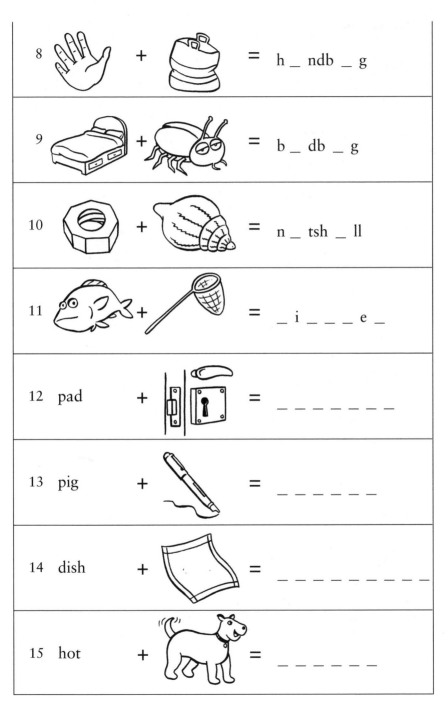

8   +   =   h _ ndb _ g

9   +   =   b _ db _ g

10   +   =   n _ tsh _ ll

11   +   =   _ i _ _ _ e _

12   pad   +   =   _ _ _ _ _ _ _

13   pig   +   =   _ _ _ _ _ _

14   dish   +   =   _ _ _ _ _ _ _ _

15   hot   +   =   _ _ _ _ _ _

C *Advanced*

---

1 Vowel inserts

Read the definition to complete each word with its correct 'short' vowels.

1 A thief or robber   b _ n d _ t

2 It could be mathematical or personal   p r _ b l e m

3 A quick meal or snack, with bread   s _ n d w _ c h

4 Vegetable for Cinderella's carriage   p _ m p k _ n

5 One more than twins   t r _ p l _ t s

6 Open footwear for the summer   s _ n d a l

7 A brass wind instrument   t r _ m p _ t

8 A competition   c _ n t _ s t

9 A serviette   n _ p k _ n

10 A tooth doctor   d _ n t _ s t

11 Created something original   _ n v _ n t e d

12 Like a devil   s a t _ n _ c

13 Big American river   M _ s s _ s s _ p p _

14 Bad behaviour   m _ s c _ n d _ c t

15 To live in   _ n h _ b _ t

© Cambridge University Press 2000

2 Compound words

Choose a word from A and find its partner in B in order to make a compound word which matches its definition below. Find at least seven.

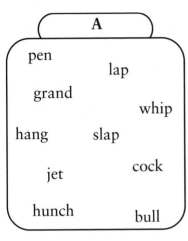

A

pen
   lap
grand
      whip
hang   slap
jet   cock
hunch   bull

B

man   frog
   stick
back   pal
   top   pit
lash   lag
stand

Definitions

1 A portable computer ....

2 A word game ....

3 Place to sit in a stadium ....

4 Famous character from Notre Dame ....

5 Low comedy form ....

6 Tiredness after a long flight ....

7 A friend you write to ....

8 A neck injury ....

9 Green creature, found near ponds ....

10 Found at the front of a plane ....

Answers

A1

1 cat　2 big　3 bed　4 pen　5 bat　6 hot　7 cup　8 dog　9 truck

A2

1 bed　2 box　3 fat　4 dog　5 ten　6 bus　7 sun　8 ship　9 frog
10 fish

A3

1 pig　2 map　3 red　4 hand　5 man　6 lips　7 fox　8 ten
9 golf　10 run　11 duck　12 hot　13 six　14 wet　15 neck
16 bad　17 dress　18 cup　19 disc　20 doll

B1

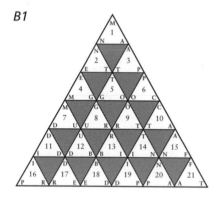

B2

1 sunset　2 windmill　3 drumstick　4 fanclub　5 lipstick
6 anthill　7 sandbox　8 handbag　9 bedbug　10 nutshell
11 fishnet　12 padlock　13 pigpen　14 dishcloth　15 hotdog

C1

1 bandit　2 problem　3 sandwich　4 pumpkin　5 triplets
6 sandal　7 trumpet　8 contest　9 napkin　10 dentist
11 invented　12 satanic　13 Mississippi　14 misconduct
15 inhabit

C2

1 laptop　2 hangman　3 grandstand　4 hunchback　5 slapstick
6 jetlag　7 penpal　8 whiplash　9 bullfrog　10 cockpit

1.2 Short and long vowels – a comparison

Lesson plan

Note:
Recognizing the difference between short and long vowels is difficult, especially when you must make a connection between the sound and the letter(s).

The exercises in this unit provide an opportunity for students of all abilities to strengthen their ability to differentiate between short and long vowel sounds on the first level: listening differentiation.

1 WRITE ON THE BOARD: Draw the following table with only the headings.

1 vowel	2 short sound	3 long sound
a	mad	made
e	red	read
i	win	wine
o	hop	hope
u	cut	cute

2 ELICIT the five vowels and write them in column 1, reviewing *orally* their short sounds in words such as **cat, bed, big, hot** and **cup.**

Then fill in the **minimal pairs** as shown in columns 2 and 3. (In these minimal pairs, the consonants remain the same but the vowel sound differs.) It is a good idea to stress the difference in the vowel sounds for each pair. *Note:* In the long vowel sound, **the vowel says its name.**

3 PRACTISE the different sounds with a short listening comprehension. Read one of each pair of words and ask the students to identify which word they hear and write it down.

4 PAIR PRACTICE: Students can 'test' each other on the same list of words. One student reads a word and the partner has to say whether the vowel is long or short.

Warm-up practice for comparing short and long vowel sounds

The following listening exercises should be done in progression with all students. You might like to adjust the vocabulary according to the level of your class.

1 Write the following pairs of words on the board for the students to copy into their notebooks. Students have to differentiate between sounds: the sound /ɪ/, as in *big* and the sound /iː/, as in *seem*. Dictate one word from each pair. Ask the students to underline the word they hear.

SHORT	LONG	SHORT	LONG
ship	sheep	kiss	keys
sit	seat	this	these
fill	feel	fit	feet
hit	heat		

2 In this exercise the students have to differentiate between five short and five long vowel sounds. Dictate one word from each pair and the students underline the word they hear.

SHORT	LONG	SHORT	LONG
bat	bait	sell	seal
rat	rate	cut	cute
bed	bead	sock	soak
pop	pope	fit	fight
sit	sight	red	read
mad	made	duck	duke
bed	bead	cot	coat
not	note	still	style

3 In this exercise the students have to differentiate between five short and five long vowel sounds. Students may work in pairs, taking turns to read out one word from each line. The partner must identify the word. For additional challenge, suggest that the identification be done within two to three minutes.

ship	shape	hat	hate
shop	sheep	heat	hit
cup	cop	mean	men
cape	cap	man	mine

duck	Dick		Tim	time
dock	duke		tame	team
pop	pipe		fit	fat
pope	pip		feet	fight
read	red		tone	ten
rod	rid		tin	tune

4 Write the following sets of words on the board for the students to copy. Working individually, students say each word quietly to themselves. If the vowel sound is short, they write *SH* above the vowel letter(s). If the vowel sound is long, they write *L*.

man	jeep	main	line
red	stand	hope	Jack
job	night	week	my
day	prize	high	boat
stone	great	wine	sad
name	coke	print	joke
mule	rose	buy	cup
pet	type	weight	twin

Their answers should look like this:

SH man	*L* jeep	*L* main	*L* line
SH red	*SH* stand	*L* hope	*SH* Jack
SH job	*L* night	*L* week	*L* my
L day	*L* prize	*L* high	*L* boat
L stone	*L* great	*L* wine	*SH* sad
L name	*L* coke	*SH* print	*L* joke
L mule	*L* rose	*L* buy	*SH* cup
SH pet	*L* type	*L* weight	*SH* twin

2 The sound 'k' (/k/)

2.1 'c' or 'k'

Lesson plan

In this unit we will study the various letters which represent or include the sound /k/ as in *cat*, *kitchen*, *black*, *picnic*, *queen* and *tax*. In this lesson we will look at words where the /k/ sound appears at the beginning or the middle of a word and is spelled with a 'c' or 'k', as in *cat* or *kitchen*.

Note:

1 In order to facilitate learning, the lesson plan and the beginner exercises concentrate on the sound /k/ at the beginning of a word. Intermediate and advanced exercises include this sound both in the beginning and middle positions.

2 The letters '-ke' are commonly found at the end of single-syllable words and after a long vowel sound produced by the Magic 'E', as in *bake* and *like*. The Magic 'E' is a pattern found in short words that end in vowel–consonant–silent 'e', where the preceding vowel will always say its own name. We include this spelling pattern in later units.

1 ELICIT: Ask students to suggest words which begin with a /k/ sound, as in *cat* and *kitchen*. Write them on the board in two columns, according to their initial letter, 'c' or 'k'.

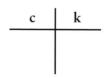

2 ASK if they see any pattern with the 'k' sounding words. Students should notice that 'e' or 'i' always follows the 'k'. What spelling pattern can we deduce from this? Note students' suggestions.

Common exceptions

You may like to point out to more advanced students that exceptions to this are words that have been 'borrowed' from other languages, like **kangaroo, karate** and **kosher**. 'ch' is another way of spelling 'k' in some English words and its etymology lies in Greek. Some examples are **school, scheme, chemist, echo** and **chorus**.

3 WRITE ON THE BOARD:

> When we hear the sound /k/ at the beginning of a
> word, write 'k' if it is followed by 'e' or 'i' and 'c'
> if followed by 'a', 'o', 'u' or a consonant.

4 EXPLAIN AND ADD: 'c' is pronounced /k/ in the middle of words when followed by 't' , for example, *act, picture, section*. When 'c' is followed by 'i', 'e' or 'y', it is pronounced /s/ as in *place, city, fancy*. This pattern is dealt with at length in Unit 9.

You might suggest that students add the relevant information to their notebooks, with examples and a separate note for exceptions.

Warm-up practice of 'c' or 'k' spelling pattern

You can use the following list of ten words which begin with 'c' or 'k' and dictate the list as a listening exercise. The same list can be used at three levels.

candle key crazy keep cold clip cup kid ketchup kind

* *Beginners* can simply write down if they think the word begins with a 'c' or a 'k'.

* *Intermediate* students can be given partially written words and then fill in the missing letters.

* *Advanced* students may write out the words on their own as they are dictated.

A Beginners

1 Sentence time

On the board, let the class make up sentences using as many 'c' and 'k' words as possible. You can start the sentence on the board, for example: A cat ...

Students can suggest any addition to the sentence of up to three words, providing one of the words begins with a /k/ sound. This activity could also be used for Intermediate students.

2 Categories

A student comes to the front of the classroom and says, for example, s/he is thinking of a vegetable which begins with a 'c' or 'k'. The class tries to guess the vegetable s/he is thinking of by asking questions. Finally, the correct vegetable (maybe 'carrot') is written on the board. This activity can also be played in pairs or groups.

Suggestions for categories:

Countries: Canada, Colombia, Kenya, Cameroon, Cuba

Fruit and vegetables: kiwi, carrot, cucumber, cabbage

Objects: candle, computer, key, kite

Animals: cat, koala, kangaroo, camel

Cities: Cambridge, Copenhagen, Cairo, Kobe

---

3 King for a day

Use the picture on the next page to find at least 18 'c' and 'k' words. You can cover up the words below to make it more difficult. Draw or write three more 'c' and 'k' words on the picture. In groups, use the picture to tell a story.

king   kettle   cat   calendar   kangaroo   cup   key   carpet
cactus   kick   candle   cage   curtain   ketchup   kite   cap
crown   clown   cable   kilt   kid   cream   coffee   kitten   car
computer   clock   canary   cloud

© Cambridge University Press 2000

B Intermediate

1 My 'c', my 'k'

In ten minutes, see how many words students can write that begin with 'c' or 'k'. Work according to the following categories:

- a place you know
- a person you like
- foods
- verbs
- things at the seaside
- different feelings
- things in the classroom
- things at home
- tools
- things you might do on holiday

2 Wordsearch

Solve the clues below the grid, write the words in the space provided and then find the words hidden within the wordsearch. Words are found from left to right and from top to bottom.

K	I	N	G	F	I	S	H	E	R	C	C
I	V	K	C	O	R	R	E	C	T	K	A
T	K	C	A	C	K	K	C	O	K	C	B
C	O	N	T	A	I	N	S	R	D	A	X
H	C	M	T	B	W	L	C	N	Z	T	C
E	A	I	L	I	I	K	I	L	L	E	R
N	N	K	E	N	N	E	L	K	C	Q	Y
K	E	N	Y	A	C	C	K	I	S	S	Q

Clues

Room to cook or bake in ....

Cows ....

Taxi ....

A New Zealand bird ....

Able – or a tin ....

To fix – that's right! ....

At sad movies you ... .

It says 'meow' ....

A place for dogs ....

Holds ....

Eat it hot and yellow ....

A fish-eating bird ....

A murderer ....

An African country ....

When two pairs of lips meet ....

A small house, made of wood ....

C Advanced

1 'c'–'k' challenge

Divide the class into groups. Each group is given one of these tasks:

- Write as many two- (or more) syllable words as you can that begin with 'k' ('ke' or 'ki').
- Write as many two- (or more) syllable words as you can that begin with 'c', or have the letter 'c' in the middle ('ca', 'co', 'cu', 'cr', 'cl', 'ct').
- Write as many words as you can that start with 'k', or have the letter 'k' in the middle, but do not follow the 'ke'/'ki' pattern.
- Write as many words as you can where 'ch' sounds like /k/.

Students can check their words in a dictionary.

Finally, the groups can present their lists to the class, allowing other students to add to the lists.

2 Building blocks

Complete the building blocks by solving the clues. Use the same letters plus one more as you go down to the middle (seven-letter) word. Rearrange the letters each time to form your new words. Remove one letter and rearrange the remaining letters as you go down from the middle word to the bottom. Hint: all words have 'c' sounding /k/ in them!

You might like to do the first clue with your teacher, to make sure you have understood.

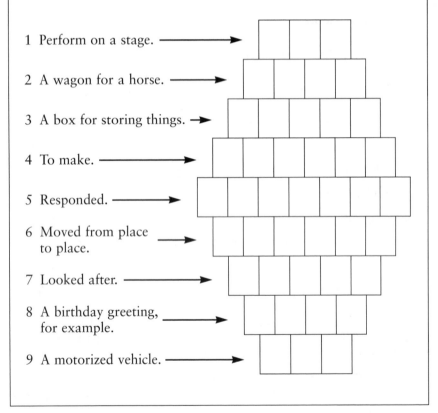

1 Perform on a stage. ⟶

2 A wagon for a horse. ⟶

3 A box for storing things. ➔

4 To make. ⟶

5 Responded. ⟶

6 Moved from place to place. ➔

7 Looked after. ⟶

8 A birthday greeting, for example. ➔

9 A motorized vehicle. ⟶

3 Step ladders

Solve the clues to the puzzle. To form the words in the B column, remove one letter from the A column and rearrange the remaining letters. Write the letter you removed in the step ladder on the left. Do the same to form the word in column C, writing the letter you removed in the step ladder on the right. Reading downwards, you will find a tasty treat in the step ladders! The first three answers have been entered for you.

		A		B		C	
c	1	crack	2	rack	3	ark	c
	4		5		6		
	7		8		9		
	10		11		12		
	13		14		15		

Clues

1 A thin line, in a cup, maybe.
2 A place to hang your hat and coat.
3 Noah's ship.
4 Player in a movie or on stage.
5 Warm outdoor wear.
6 Bed for baby.
7 'Stopper' on a car or bike.
8 Noise a dog makes.
9 Pub; place for drinking.
10 Machines for taking photos.
11 Thick, sweet milk products.
12 Go away! Shoo!
13 Expensive furs.
14 It covers your body.
15 Writing fluid in a pen.

The sound 'k' (/k/)

Suggested words for spelling test

1 *Beginners*

clip	kid	can	cop	king
camp	kitten	cat	class	Ken

2 *Intermediate*

kitchen	camera	club	computer	command
collar	custom	card	coffee	kettle
kind	capital	kingdom	connect	key

3 *Advanced*

cartoon	classify	craft	critical	kennel
kindness	common	consider	contact	kindergarten
crash	crossing	conflict	keyring	canary

Answers

B2

K	I	N	G	F	I	S	H	E	R	C	C
I	V	K	C	O	R	R	E	C	T	K	A
T	K	C	A	C	K	K	C	O	K	C	B
C	O	N	T	A	I	N	S	R	D	A	X
H	C	M	T	B	W	L	C	N	Z	T	C
E	A	I	L	I	I	K	I	L	L	E	R
N	N	K	E	N	N	E	L	K	C	Q	Y
K	E	N	Y	A	C	C	K	I	S	S	Q

Clues

Room to cook or bake in – kitchen

Cows – cattle

Taxi – cab

A New Zealand bird – kiwi

Able – or a tin – can

To fix – that's right! – correct

At sad movies you ... – cry
It says 'meow' – cat
A place for dogs – kennel
Holds – contains
Eat it hot and yellow – corn
A fish-eating bird – kingfisher
A murderer – killer
An African country – Kenya
When two pairs of lips meet – kiss
A small house, made of wood – cabin

C2

1 act   2 cart   3 crate   4 create   5 reacted   6 carted   7 cared
8 card   9 car

C3

	A	B	C	
c	1 crack	2 rack	3 ark	c
r	4 actor	5 coat	6 cot	a
e	7 brake	8 bark	9 bar	k
a	10 cameras	11 creams	12 scram	e
m	13 minks	14 skin	15 ink	s

2.2 '-ck' or '-k' at the end of a word

Lesson plan

Note:
This lesson looks at the sound /k/ at the end of a single-syllable word, when it is written '-ck' or '-k', as in *black* and *think*.

1 WRITE ON THE BOARD:

-ck	-k	-k
black	bank	book
neck	mask	week
stick	dark	speak
clock	talk	

2 ELICIT: Have the students compare the words in the three lists. Students should notice that what they have in common is that they all end in the letter 'k' and are one-syllable words. They are different because a short, single vowel precedes '-ck', and a consonant ('n', 's', 'r' or 'l') or two vowel letters precede '-k'. For advanced students you may want to mention this pattern also applies to 'oak' words, as in *croak*.

3 WRITE ON THE BOARD:

-ck

> We write '-ck' at the end of a single-syllable
> word which has a short vowel sound.
> -ack -eck -ick -ock -uck

-k

> We write '-k' at the end of a single-syllable
> word, when it is preceded by 'n', 's', 'r' or 'l' or
> by two vowel letters.

You might suggest that students add this to their notebooks, with examples.

Warm-up practice of '-k' and '-ck' spelling pattern

You may want to concentrate separately on '-ck' and then add '-k', or mix them both together. There are, therefore, two simple listening exercises.

You can use the following list of words which end in '-k' or '-ck' and dictate ten of the words as a listening exercise. The same list can be used at three levels.

> trick speak cracker cheek dark duck sticker packing truck cook ask bank shark black milk park look track Greek sack

* *Beginners* and *intermediate* students can write '-k' or '-ck' according to what they have learnt this lesson.

* *Advanced* students can write the words as they are read out.

A Beginners

1 Pantomime

Prepare 20 or more '-ck' and '-k' words on cards and put them into a bag. Divide the class into two teams. Representatives of both teams send an 'actor' to pick a wordcard from the bag. The first team to guess and correctly spell the word mimed by the actor gets a point.

Suggested '-ck' words: *back, clock, lucky, sock, duck, jacket, kick, lick, lock, truck, quickly, black, hockey, brick, trick, stick.*

Suggested '-k' words: *milk, talk, walk, mask, tank, sink, pink, think, shark, bark, dark, chalk, cheek, week, look, cook, speak, weak.*

2 Spelling Olympics

Divide the class into groups. Give them ten minutes to make as many words as possible that follow the '-ck' and '-k' patterns. The winning team has the best total. Help the teams by writing on the board:

> -ack -eck -ick -ock -uck -nk -sk -lk -nk -ook
> -eek -eak

3 Picture identification

See the Intermediate section. Find at least seven.

B *Intermediate*

1 *Fun with k*

This exercise uses only words that end in 'k' and are preceded by two vowels. Add two vowels to complete the table in order to solve the clues. You will need 'OO', 'OA', 'EE' and 'EA'. If you are stuck, use a dictionary to help. Find at least eight.

Clue					
Something to read.		B			K
A coat with no sleeves.	C	L			K
Peter Pan's enemy: Captain … .		H			K
The noise of a frog.	C	R			K
Past of 'take'.		T			K
Moved up and down quickly.	S	H			K
'Mouth' of a bird.		B			K
Homer spoke this.	G	R			K
Seven days.		W			K
On each side of your face.	C	H			K
A chef.		C			K
To talk or say.	S	P			K
To see.		L			K

© Cambridge University Press 2000

2 Picture identification

Write the number of the word by its correct picture (Example: A – 18). Do at least 15. To make it more difficult, look at the pictures without the word list and write the correct word next to each picture. Then try to add one more word that uses this rule and is connected to the picture by association, for example, lock – stuck.

Word list

1 book	2 blackboard	3 desk	4 socks
5 milk	6 shark	7 clock	8 sack
9 lock	10 ink	11 rocking chair	12 sick
13 bark	14 duck	15 parking	16 hockey stick
17 mask	18 hook	19 tank	20 suck

C Advanced

1 Play it '-ck'

Find as many words as you can from the list. All the words end in '-ck'.

1 It tells the time. ....

2 Two boy's names. ....

3 You put them on your feet. ....

4 A bird that likes to swim. ....

5 Another name for a dress. ....

6 Fast. ....

7 You do this to an ice cream. ....

8 Not the front. ....

9 A big stone. ....

10 A colour. ....

11 A lorry. ....

12 A group of sheep. ....

13 A dollar, or a male deer. ....

14 To make fun of. ....

15 A long, thin piece of wood. ....

16 A place for ships to land. ....

17 A male chicken. ....

18 You build houses with them. ....

© Cambridge University Press 2000

19 To hit somebody. ....

20 To close with a key. ....

Now find FOUR more words that end in '-ck', and make up your own clues for them ...

21 ....

22 ....

23 ....

24 ....

---

2 Dictionary work

Use your dictionary in order to answer these questions about '-ck' and '-k' words. Find at least 11.

1 What might you find tied to a dock?

2 What kind of person is a 'peacock'?

3 What do the British call 'crackers'?

4 Why do horses wear 'blinkers'?

5 Who are the 'rank' and file?

6 What does a 'husky' voice sound like?

7 Why is 'caulking' a boat important?

8 What jumps out of a jack-in-the-box?

9 How much money is a 'nickel'?

10 What part of a horse's body are its 'flanks'?

11 What would you find in a 'flock'?

12 Where can you buy 'stocks' and shares?

13 What kind of a person is a 'brick'?

14 Why would you need a 'jack' for your car?

15 What time of the day is 'dusk'?

The sound 'k' (/k/)

3 Crossword

The answers to all the clues in this crossword are words from Lesson 1 of this unit ('c'/'k') and '-k'.

ACROSS

1 A room where you can cook and bake.
3 A chance; something dangerous.
6 The person who makes you laugh at 2 down.
7 Sleeps (slang).
8 It covers your whole body.
10 A taxi.
12 Able – or a tin.
13 To perform on the stage.
15 An Australian bear.
16 To weep (tears from your eyes).
17 What you have to do to complete this crossword.

DOWN

1 A place for a dog to sleep.
2 Big tent entertainment.
3 Where to skate.
4 To jump with rope.
5 Funny – like 6 across.
9 If your pen leaks, your fingers are … .
11 A safe place for money.
14 It says 'Meow!'

40

Suggested words for spelling test

The lists include words from previously learnt rules.

1 *Beginners*

black	ask	drink	clock	kick
park	walk	speak	pink	cook

2 *Intermediate*

bark	sticker	packing	cracker	bookmark
looking	hockey	weakness	hooked	blacken
chicken	market	asking	brick	junk

3 *Advanced*

peacock	nickel	flocking	cracked	backwards
thickness	shrink	silk	task	clerk
homesick	wicked	risky	darkness	stockmarket

Answers

B1

1 book   2 cloak   3 Hook   4 croak   5 took   6 shook   7 beak
8 Greek   9 week   10 cheek   11 cook   12 speak   13 look

B2

A–18   B–6   C–2   D–5   E–11   F–17   G–19   H–14   I–8
J–9   K–16   L–7   M–1   N–10   O–15   P–13   Q–20
R–4   S–12   T–3

C1

1 clock   2 Jack, Mick   3 socks   4 duck   5 frock   6 quick   7 lick
8 back   9 rock   10 black   11 truck   12 flock   13 buck
14 mock   15 stick   16 dock   17 cock   18 bricks   19 smack
20 lock

C2

Possible answers
1 A boat or ship.
2 A proud person, one who likes to dress showily.
3 Dry biscuits, often eaten with butter or another spread.
4 So they won't be distracted.
5 Regular soldiers in an army.

6 Deep, with emotion.
7 It will make it watertight.
8 A clown on a spring.
9 Five (American) cents.
10 The side, between its ribs and hip.
11 A lot of birds, sheep or ...
12 On the Stock Exchange.
13 A good-hearted one.
14 To lift it, in order to change a punctured tyre.
15 Evening, when the sun goes down.

C3

¹K	I	T	²C	H	E	N			
E			I			³R	I	⁴S	K
N			R	⁵C		I		K	
N		⁶C	L	O	W	N		I	
E			U		M		⁷K	I	P	S
L			⁸S	K	I	N			
		⁹I			C			¹⁰C	A	¹¹B
¹²C	A	N			¹³A	¹⁴C	T			A
		¹⁵K	O	A	L	A			N
¹⁶C	R	Y				¹⁷T	H	I	N	K

2.3 '-ic'

Lesson plan

Note:
Since the vocabulary level of words that end in '-ic' is for intermediate and advanced students, most of the exercises for this spelling pattern are at these levels. However, we feel that it is important for all students to know that when they hear the sound /ɪk/ as in *panic* at the end of a multi-syllable word, it will be written as '-ic'.

1 RECALL: What is a syllable? (from Unit 1). A quick way to do this is by tapping out or clapping the divisions of the names of some students in the class and of long words that are familiar to them, for example, John-a-than, E-liz-a-beth, class-room.

  Recall '-ck' from the previous lesson. Words that end in '-ick' have only one syllable.

2 ELICIT: Ask students to suggest words that have two or more syllables and end in the sound /ɪk/. Write them on the board.

3 ASK: What spelling pattern can we deduce from this? Note students' suggestions.

4 WRITE ON THE BOARD:

> We write '-ic' when we hear the sound /ɪk/
> at the end of a word that has two or
> more syllables.

You might suggest that students add this to their notebooks, with examples.

Warm-up practice of '-ic' spelling pattern

The same list can be used at two levels. Choose ten words from the following list and dictate them as a listening exercise. It is recommended to include some '-ick' words from the previous lesson.

plastic fantastic trick logic electric clinic thick traffic
chick arithmetic stick Mick Atlantic click brick
classic magic

* *Beginners* and *intermediate* students can write either '-ic' if the word they hear has more that one syllable, or '-ick' if it has only one syllable.

* *Advanced* students can write the whole word they hear.

A Beginners

1 Mission possible

This is a game for two to four players. You need a die and counters or buttons. Make copies of the game and stick them on to cardboard. Each player throws the die. The player who throws the highest number goes first. In turn, throw the die and move the counter to the right place. The winner is the student who finishes first.

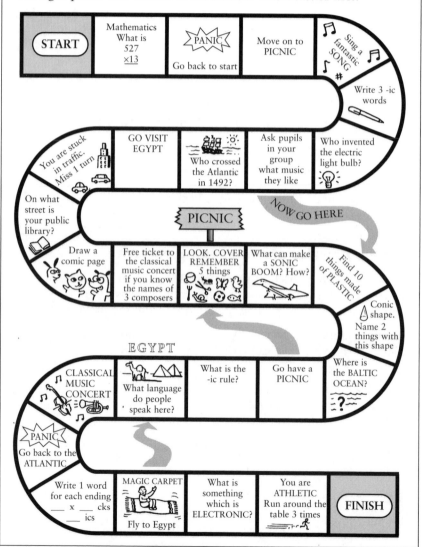

B Intermediate

1 Word pairs

Match '-ic' words with nouns to form common phrases and idiomatic expressions. Do it as a competition between groups, to see who gets the most logical pairings within three minutes.

traffic	festival
picnic	band
elastic	boom
metric	basket
magic	clock
sonic	circle
Arctic	system
Atlantic	lights
music	ocean
electric	stick

© Cambridge University Press 2000

2 What's their line?

Match fields of work with phrases that describe professions. All the fields of work end in '-ics'. A dictionary might be useful here to look up some of the words in the word bank. Do at least ten. The first one has been done for you. (A * means that this is difficult, so be careful!)

PROFESSION	FIELD OF WORK
1 An acrobat in a circus	*acrobatics*
2 A Member of Parliament	
3 A beautician in a store	
4 A scientist of DNA and heredity	
5 A person who studies language	
6 A robot builder	
7 A runner on a sportstrack	
8 An expert in aircrafts and flight	
9 A person who studies drawing	
10 A person who fixes cars or tractors	
11 A scientist of matter and energy	
12 A doctor of children's illnesses *	
13 A specialist in old age *	

Word bank:

acrobatics   aeronautics   athletics   cosmetics   genetics
geriatrics   graphics   linguistics   mechanics   pediatrics
physics   politics   robotics

C Advanced

1 Words in the circle

a. All the words in the circle below end in '-ic'. See if you can find eight of them. The first letter of each word is capitalized in each segment. Write the words you find on the lines.

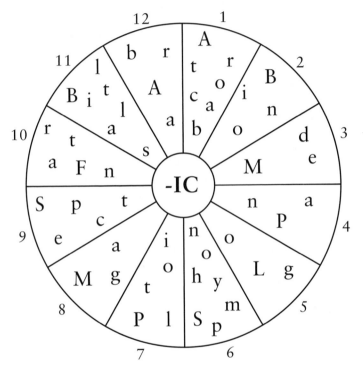

1 ....

2 ....

3 ....

4 ....

5 ....

6 ....

7 ....

8 ....

9 ....

10 ....

11 ....

12 ....

b. Use ten words from the previous exercise to fill in the blanks with an appropriate word.

1 *The* .... *Flute* was composed by Mozart.

2 The Prime Minister knows a lot about .... s.

3 Keep cool – don't ....

4 My father was .... when he discovered that he had lost his car keys.

5 A scud is a kind of .... missile.

6 Someone who has studied basic medicine is a ....

7 A .... is someone who doubts.

8 It is not ....al to put ice cream in the oven.

9 The most common language spoken in Jordan
   is ....

10 An .... person can put his feet on his shoulders.

2 Making adjectives

Each of the words in the following list can be used to form '-ic' adjectives. Find at least ten adjectives. A dictionary will be useful here to check spelling.

After you finish finding the '-ic' adjectives, add a noun of your choice to each, for example, 'fantastic experience'. In pairs, explain to your partner why you have chosen this particular noun.

NOUN	'-IC' ADJECTIVE	NOUN PHRASE
1 fantasy	....	....
2 gymnasium	....	....
3 science	....	....
4 gene	....	....
5 Hebrew	....	....
6 Celt	....	....
7 German	....	....
8 state	....	....
9 graph	....	....
10 barbarian	....	....
11 metal	....	....
12 analysis	....	....
13 problem	....	....
14 scene	....	....
15 symphony	....	....

Suggested words for spelling tests

The lists include words from previously learnt rules.

1 *Intermediate*

garlic	fantastic	kilt	rink	panic
stuck	magic	crack	logic	basic
task	rock	park	crab	tactic

2 *Advanced*

optimistic	domestic	Pacific	bunkbed	trickster
lacking	sympathetic	poetic	stocking	weekend
satanic	classical	pocketbook	magical	tragic

Answers

B1

We found the following phrases and expressions: you may find more.

traffic lights, traffic circle, traffic system
picnic basket
elastic band
metric system
magic stick, magic festival, magic circle
sonic boom
Arctic Circle, Arctic Ocean
Atlantic Ocean
music festival
electric clock, electric lights

B2

Note:
You might want to draw your students' attention to the fact that all these fields of work are singular nouns, although they look like plurals, which means that we say: 'politics **is**' and not 'politics **are**'.

1 acrobatics   2 politics   3 cosmetics   4 genetics   5 linguistics
6 robotics   7 athletics   8 aeronautics   9 graphics   10 mechanics
11 physics   12 pediatrics   13 geriatrics

C1a

1 acrobatic   2 bionic   3 medic   4 panic   5 logic   6 symphonic
7 politic   8 magic   9 sceptic   10 frantic   11 ballistic   12 Arabic

C1b

1 Magic   2 politic   3 panic   4 frantic   5 ballistic   6 medic
7 sceptic   8 logic   9 Arabic   10 acrobatic

C2

1 fantastic   2 gymnastic   3 scientific   4 genetic   5 Hebraic
6 Celtic   7 Germanic   8 static   9 graphic   10 barbaric
11 metallic   12 analytic   13 problematic   14 scenic
15 symphonic

2.4 'qu'

Lesson plan

Note:
This lesson looks at the sound /kw/ as in *quick*. This is a common spelling pattern and is found at the beginning or in the middle of words. The letter 'q' is always followed by 'u' and another vowel.

1   RECALL: What are the letter patterns that we have learnt that give us the sound /k/? Answer: 'c' as in *cat*, 'k' as in *kettle*, '-ck' as in *back*, and '-ic' as in *magic*.

2   ASK: How do the following word pairs differ in the sound /k/?

   queen – keen   quite – kite   square – scare   squid – skid

   Answer: The first word of each pair has the sound /kw/ and the second the sound /k/.

3   WRITE ON THE BOARD: It might be a good idea to write up the minimal pairs from the previous task and get the students to practise saying them.

4   ASK: What spelling pattern can we deduce from this? Note students' suggestions.

5 WRITE ON THE BOARD:

> When we hear the sound /kw/ in a word, we write 'qu'. 'Q' never stands alone: it is always followed by 'u' + vowel.

You might suggest that students write this in their notebooks.

Warm-up practice of 'qu' spelling pattern

You can choose ten words from the following list and dictate them as a listening exercise. The same list can be used at two levels. It is recommended to include words from the previous lessons.

clap   trick   quit   black   shock   crown   square   drink
care   jack   quarrel   question   picnic   snack   quiz   dark
quick   king   cross

* *Beginners* and *intermediate* students can write 'c', 'k', '-ck', '-ic' or 'qu'.

* *Advanced* students can write the whole word.

A Beginners

---

1 Picture quiz

In order to find the word in Column 3, look at the picture in Column 1 and unscramble the letters in Column 2.

1	2	3
1	a r o q e u t	equator
2	o n q t e s u i	
3	n q u e e	

© Cambridge University Press 2000

4	k u c d	....
5	s r q e u a	....
6	q r u u a i a m	....
7	z i q u	....

8	i
	      k
	  d
		....

9	t r r q e u a	....
10	n d c y a	....

2 Find out ...

1 ... which kid in your class asks the most questions.

2 ... when your next quiz is.

3 ... which Egyptian queen fell in love with Anthony.

4 ... five different things you can put in an aquarium.

5 ... the names of five games or sports where you have to run
quickly.

B Intermediate

1 Letter-fill

Complete the letters in the diagram according to the clues on the left. Do at least seven.

1	It has 4 equal sides		Q	U						
2	The same for everyone		Q	U						
3	A furry animal with a long tail		Q	U						
4	Zero degrees latitude		Q	U						
5	?		Q	U						
6	Fast		Q	U						
7	A test		Q	U						
8	A place for fish at home		Q	U						
9	The king's wife		Q	U						
10	$\frac{1}{4}$		Q	U						

2 Qu – trivia

a. As an oral exercise, your teacher will give both the definition and the choices. Write down or respond orally with the correct 'qu' word.
OR:
b. As individual or pair work, find the word which fits the definition from the offered choices. Use dictionaries to help where necessary. Do at least nine.

1 To make a noise like a mouse. (*quiz, queer, squeak*)

2 Another word for an argument. (*quarrel, equal, equipment*)

3 A small red or grey furry animal with a big tail. It likes nuts. (*quotation, squirrel, quest*)

4 An earth-moving experience is a … (*queen, aquarium, quake*)

5 To press very hard on somebody or something from all sides is to … (*quarter, squeak, squeeze*)

6 A flat form with four sides of the same length. (*square, squirrel, quake*)

7 'To be or not to be' is a famous … from Shakespeare's *Hamlet*. (*earthquake, quotation, squeeze*)

8 After a murder, the police always carry out an … (*inquisition, inquest, aquarium*)

9 Zero degrees latitude. (*equator, quarrel, quest*)

10 A line of people waiting for something. (*queue, squeeze, quote*)

C *Advanced*

1 Bull's eye

Starting at the bull's eye (centre) of each target, work outwards, taking one letter or letter cluster from each ring to form correct English words. For example, in the first target, it is possible to spell **QU-O-T-E**. How many words can you find?

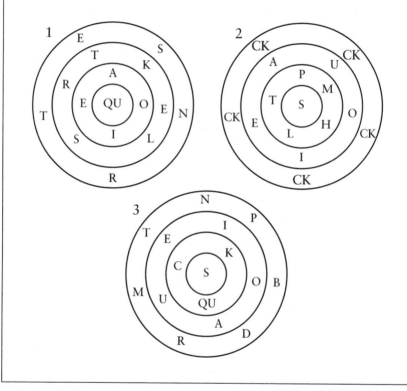

2 Compound words

From the word bank, match a word to those below to make compound words or familiar phrases. Most of the words will be used more than once. A dictionary will be useful. Do at least 15.

Word bank:

Queen   country   question   quarter   aqua
quick   square   skin

1 ....'s English

2 to pop the ....

3 'Beauty is only .... deep'

4 .... mother

5 four ....s of the moon

6 .... silver

7 .... master

8 .... music

9 .... of an hour

10 .... dancing

11 thick ....

12 .... marine

13 .... back

14 .... mark

15 .... lung

16 .... house

17 .... sands

18 a .... meal

19 .... thinking

20 a .... of time

© Cambridge University Press 2000

Suggested words for spelling test

The lists include words from previously learnt rules.

1 *Beginners*

quick	kit	magic	kind	car
queen	quiet	tank	quiz	clinic

2 *Intermediate*

question	traffic	queer	careful	skin
quickly	squash	problematic	square	energetic
clock	quack	key	stink	quit

3 *Advanced*

catholic	quality	equip	keel	skill
aquatic	critic	shrink	wicked	cricket
squirrel	equator	conduct	risky	kennel

Answers

A1

1 equator   2 question   3 queen   4 duck   5 square   6 aquarium
7 quiz   8 kid   9 quarter   10 candy

B1

1 square   2 equality   3 squirrel   4 equator   5 question   6 quick
7 quiz   8 aquarium   9 queen   10 quarter

B2

1 squeak   2 quarrel   3 squirrel   4 quake   5 squeeze
6 square   7 quotation   8 inquest   9 equator   10 queue

C1

1 quite, quote, queen, quake, quart, queer, quits, quest, quilt.

2 smack, stack, stick, stuck, stock, slack, slick, shack, shock.
  Bonus words (very hard): spick, smock.

3 squad, skin, skip, skit, skim, scot, scan, scud, scar.
  Bonus words (very hard): squid, squib, scab, scam.

C2

1	Queen's English	
2	to pop the question	
3	'Beauty is only skin deep'	
4	Queen mother	
5	four quarters of the moon	
6	quick silver	
7	quarter master	
8	country music	
9	quarter of an hour	
10	square dancing	
11	thick skin	
12	aqua marine	
13	quarter back	
14	question mark	
15	aqua lung	
16	country house	
17	quick sands	
18	a square meal	
19	quick thinking	
20	a question of time	

2.5 '-x'

Lesson plan

Note:

The letter 'x' appears at the end of a syllable or a word. At the end of a word its sound is always /ks/ as in *six*. With words that begin with 'ex', its sound is either /ks/ as in *exercise* or /gz/ as in *exhibit*.

The sound /ks/ at the end of the words can be spelled in four different ways: 'ks' as in *thinks*; 'cks' as in *sticks*; 'ics' as in *comics*; and 'x' as in *six*. However, note that all words that end in 'x' are root words.

1 WRITE ON THE BOARD: Write the following column headings and examples:

EX-	MIDDLE	END OF ROOT WORD
excellent	taxi	six
extra	sixty	fax
example	text	mix

2 ASK: What sound does the letter 'x' make and what kind of vowel sound precedes it? Elicit the answers that the letter 'x' makes the sound /ks/ (or /gz/ in some 'ex-' words) and it is always preceded by a single-letter, short vowel sound.

You might like to point out that words such as *books*, *rocks*, *banks*, *takes*, *picnics* also have the sound /ks/ because these are root words plus a suffix. In words that end in 'x', we need to add 'es':

mix + es = mixes   fax + es = faxes

3 WRITE ON THE BOARD:

> If we hear /ks/ at the end of a syllable or a root word and it is preceded by a single-letter, short vowel sound, we write 'x'.

You might wish to mention to more advanced classes that the same sound /ks/ is found in 'cc' words, such as *accident* and *eccentric*.

You might suggest that students write this in their notebooks.

Warm-up practice of '-x' spelling pattern

* Beginners
You can use the seven words below as a listening-writing exercise.
Read out the words and ask the students to write them.

six box fox mix fax next sixty

* Intermediate and advanced
The following list includes words that follow the '-x' pattern as well as
'-xes', '-cks', '-ks' and '-ics' words. Read out the words and ask the
students to write them.

taxi example boxes backs picnics relax exit banks
exam politics

A Beginners

1 Initial fun

This is your chance to learn some new 'x' words. Take the first
letter from each drawing, add an 'x' to the letters to form a word
that answers the question. Write the letters on the spaces.

1 What is a candle made of?

X   = <u>W</u> <u>A</u> <u>X</u>

2 What do you do if you break a window?

X   = _ _ _ it.

3 What do you do with eggs, flour and sugar to make a cake?

X   = _ _ _ them.

© Cambridge University Press 2000

60

4 Which smart wild animal looks like a dog?

      X   = __ __ __

5 What looks like a pipe and makes music?

    X   = __ __ __

6 What word means 'This way out'?

 X   = __ __ __ __

7 What can you put things in?

   X   = __ __ __

8 How do you send a note by phone?

      X   = __ __ __ __ it.

9 What car do you pay to ride in?

  X    = __ __ __ __

10 What is like a quiz?

 X    = __ __ __ __

2 The crazy millionaire's shopping list

a. Do you know what the crazy millionaire wants to buy? Look at his shopping list and fill in the '-x', '-ck' and '-k' words in place of the numbers and pictures. You can use the word bank to help you.

b. In pairs, decide what he is going to do with the things he buys. Which would he need for ... transport? ... the kitchen? ... amusement? ... work? Defend your decisions!

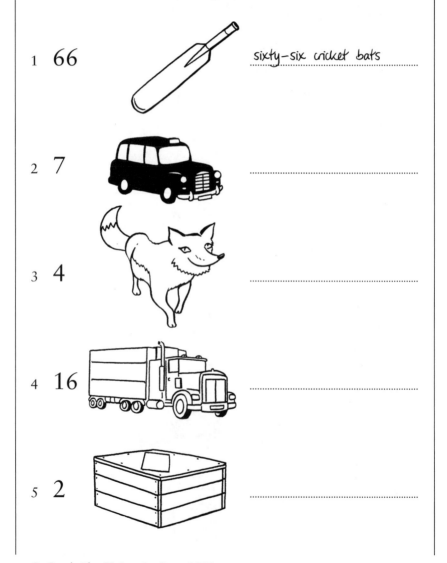

1 66   *sixty-six cricket bats*

2 7

3 4

4 16

5 2

© Cambridge University Press 2000

6 5 ....

7 1 ....

8 3 ....

9 6 ....

sixty-six   mixers   foxes   one   trucks

six   seven   fax machines   five   sixteen

boxes   two   saxophone   taxis

cricket bats   four   three   banks

© Cambridge University Press 2000

B Intermediate

1 Poet's corner

Now is your chance to become a famous poet. Complete this silly rhyme with words that end in 'x'. If you need any help, look at the words in the previous exercises.

I once had a f _ _

That sat on a b _ _ .

I called him M _ _

And he liked to r _ _ _ _ .

One day, at s _ _

I had to f _ _

My father's s _ _ .

It needed w _ _ .

M _ _ saw the s _ _

And couldn't r _ _ _ _ .

He jumped off his b _ _

And I lost my f _ _ !

© Cambridge University Press 2000

2 Letter fill-ins

a. Listen to these sentences then fill in the missing letters of the words. Use 'qu', 'ex', 'k', 'c', 'ks', 'x', 'ck', 'xes' and 'cks'.

1 The si.......... fo.......... ....it ....ercising because they felt

si.......... .

2 ....en, the sa..........ophone player, ...an't find an ....cuse

for playing ....tra notes.

3 ....itty tal.......... si..........ty words a se..........ond. That's ....ite

..........ick. In fa..........t, it's faster than a fa.......... .

b. Make up some more sentences or words with similar missing letters and give them to a friend to solve.

C Advanced

1 Dictionary definitions

Complete the sentences to show that you understand the meaning of the 'x' words. Use a dictionary to help you.

1 A dyslexic person is someone who ...

....

2 An exciting trip is one where ...

....

3 An excellent meal might consist of ...

....

4 A complex problem is one that ...

....

5 An expert is a person who ...

....

6 A galaxy contains ...

....

7 A fax is a message that ...

....

8 A hex may be used by ...

....

9 A sexist is a person who ...

....

10 If you exalt someone you ...

....

11 At an exhibition you might see ...

....

12 Latex is ...

....

13 Wax is used to make ...

....

14 A prefix is one or more letters that ...

....

15 A suffix is one or more letters that ...

....

2 Exclusive alphabet

In pairs, students work through the alphabet, writing down a word containing the letter 'x' for as many initial letters as possible, for example, axe / box. Do this within five minutes. Compare answers.

Suggested words for spelling test

The lists include words from previously learnt rules.

1 *Beginners*

sock	boxes	quick	sixty	think
clinic	fax	track	ask	mixer

2 *Intermediate*

exact	quiet	pick-up	queen	wicked
explore	wax	exit	sonic	energetic
question	exam	politics	relax	weeks

3 *Advanced*

prefix	domestic	exercise	blank	example
mixture	quarter	quest	expand	background
suffix	quality	stocking	medical	critic

Answers

A1

1 wax   2 fix   3 mix   4 fox   5 sax   6 exit   7 box   8 fax
9 taxi   10 exam

A2a

1 sixty-six cricket bats   2 seven taxis   3 four foxes   4 sixteen trucks
5 two boxes   6 five fax machines   7 one saxophone   8 three mixers
9 six banks

B1

The missing words are:
fox, box, Max, relax, six, fix, sax, wax, Max, sax, relax, box, fox

B2a

1 The six foxes quit exercising because they felt sick.
2 Ken, the saxophone player, can't find an excuse for playing extra notes.
3 Kitty talks sixty words a second. That's quite quick. In fact, it's faster than a fax.

C1

Possible answers:

 1 A dyslexic person is someone who has difficulty reading.
 2 An exciting trip is one where you have a lot of fun.
 3 An excellent meal might consist of goose, caviar and ice cream.
 4 A complex problem is one that is very hard to solve.
 5 An expert is a person who knows a lot about the subject.
 6 A galaxy contains billions of stars.
 7 A fax is a message that is sent by a special machine through a telephone.
 8 A hex may be used by a witch to turn a prince into a frog.
 9 A sexist is a person who believes that members of one sex are less intelligent than those of the other sex.
10 If you exalt someone you praise them highly.
11 At an exhibition you might see paintings and sculptures.
12 Latex is used to make rubber or glue.
13 Wax is used to make candles.
14 A prefix is one or more letters that come in front of a root word.
15 A suffix is one or more letters that come at the end of a root word.

3   Single vowel followers

3.1 '-ll', '-ss' ('-ff', '-zz')

Lesson plan

In this unit we will study various spelling patterns that come at the end of single-syllable words, preceded by a short vowel sound. This lesson looks at '-ll', '-ss', '-ff' and '-zz'. Words ending in '-ff' and '-zz' are few in number. We suggest you teach these as needed. Examples: *off, staff, stiff, cliff, buzz, jazz.*

Note:
There is a different pronunciation for 'a' in 'a+ll' words. The sound is /ɔːl/, as in *ball*. This is because the letter 'l' has a special effect on the preceding 'a'. Similarly, there is a different pronunciation of 'a' in 'a+ss' words in some dialects: *class* is pronounced /klaːss/ in some parts of England but /klæss/ in some other dialects.

1 ELICIT: Ask students to suggest one-syllable, one-vowel letter words that end with the sound /l/.

Write the words, in column form, on the board. Possible examples:

ball   tall   doll   pill   still   full   bull

Now ask students for one-syllable, one-vowel letter words that end in the sound /s/.
  Write the words on the board in a second column. Possible examples:

class   dress   miss   floss   fuss

Common exceptions

If the following words are suggested, you might like to write them in a third column, since they are words that do not follow the spelling pattern and can be taught as needed:

bus   us   yes   gas   this   plus   pal

Note the spelling of *has*, where the final 's' is pronounced /z/ (as with *gas* in some dialects).

2 ASK: What spelling pattern can we deduce from this? Note students' suggestions.

3 WRITE ON THE BOARD:

> We write '-ll' or '-ss' at the end of a
> single-syllable word, preceded by one vowel letter.
>
> -all   -ell   -ill   -oll   -ull
>
> -ass   -ess   -iss   -oss   -uss

You may want to point out to your students that the '-ll' spelling pattern does not apply to words that have more than one syllable, for example, *pencil, local, travel, towel.* The same applies if we add the suffix '-ful', which has only one 'l', for example, *beautiful* and *helpful.* This spelling pattern will be covered in a later unit.

You might suggest that students add this to their notebooks, with examples and a separate note for exceptions.

4 REMIND AND REVIEW: At this point, review the '-ck' pattern that was studied in Unit 2, which follows a similar pattern of a letter cluster that comes after a single vowel, in words such as *black, neck, sick, block, duck.*

5 ASK students if they know how to form plurals and Present Simple third person singular (he, she, it) with words that end with '-ss'. Write their answers on the board, i.e. add '-es' to these words, for example, he/she/it *kisses, presses, misses*, and for nouns, *dresses, classes, losses.*

Warm-up practice of '-ll' and '-ss' spelling pattern

The purpose of these listening exercises is to reinforce the aural differentiation between short and long vowel sounds. Some classes will not need the review, so you may want to go straight on to the written exercises. Here, the words all end in the sound /l/ or /s/. Because this exercise concentrates on the vowel sounds, students should not have to worry about knowing meanings of all the words. From the following pairs of words, choose those that are most suitable for your class and write them on the board:

heel – hell   mill – mile   bass – base   seal – sell   will – while
feel – fell   rose – Ross   fill – file   chess – cheese   pill – pile

Now continue with one of these listening activities:

* *Beginners*
Choose one of the words of each minimal pair to say aloud to the
class. Tell the student to write SHORT if the word they hear has a short
vowel sound, or LONG if they hear a long vowel sound. This may be
done in their mother tongue.

* *Intermediate and advanced*
Choose one of the words of each minimal pair to say aloud to the
class. Students write the words they hear.

* *All levels*
With a partner, students take turns to choose five minimal pairs. They
say one word from each pair and the partner must spell the word out
loud.

A Beginners

1 Picture scramble

In the following squares are pictures of words that follow the '-ss'
and '-ll' pattern. Unscramble the mixed-up letters and write the
correct words under the pictures.

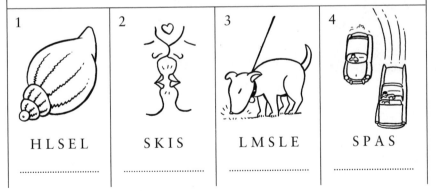

1	2	3	4
H L S E L	S K I S	L M S L E	S P A S
....	....	....	....

© Cambridge University Press 2000

5

LSGAS

....

6

OSBS

....

7

LBAL

....

8

RSGAS

....

9

ELBL

....

10

LIPL

....

11

SLAML

....

12

SHCES

....

13

LUBL

....

14

SRSDE

....

15

LSACS

....

16

LAWL

....

---

2 Trivia

Use the unscrambled words from the boxes in exercise 1 to complete these sentences:

1 You find it by the sea. ....

2 Three words that take '-es' for plural. ....

3 This person tells you what to do. ....

4 Three verbs. ....

5 You may hear it at school or on a cat. ....

6 A girl or woman may wear it. ....

7 Not big. ....

8 Something green, that cows like to eat. ....

9 A room at school. ....

10 A thinking game. ....

© Cambridge University Press 2000

B Intermediate and advanced

Note:
These exercises include '-ff' as well as '-ss' and '-ll' words. The first two exercises are based on the same picture grid.

---

1 Picture match

Match the words to the pictures in the grid.

Word bank:

puff spill glass chess ball grass ass hell staff
kiss cliff dress wall hill sell class shell doll
well bell

Single vowel followers

2 Kimberly's game

This activity is a variation of 'Kim's Game'. Look at the pictures from the grid in the previous activity for two minutes. Cover them and try to write down as many names of the pictures that you remember within two minutes – you will probably only remember five to seven words. Working with a partner, check your word list and spelling, then pool your lists together. Pair up with another couple in order to compare and add to your lists. Finally, see which group has managed to remember the most words.

3 Double trivia

The answers to all these clues are words that end either with '-ll', '-ss' or '-ff'. See how many of them you can find.

1 A mountain that ends in the sea. ....

2 A window is made of this. ....

3 Contact between two pairs of lips. ....

4 To make a hole with an electric tool. ....

5 Material; things. ....

6 Sick, not well. ....

7 It's round, bounces and is often made of rubber. ....

8 The sign of Christianity. ....

9 A board game between two armies. ....

10 The person in charge. ....

11 Not more. ....

12 To iron. ....

13 A feather pen, used many years ago. ....

14 The bottom of a shirt sleeve. ....

15 Not on. ....

16 Not empty. ....

17 A place to grind flour. ....

18 It's green and often in the garden. ....

19 A bad odour. ....

20 A sea bird. ....

21 What you have to pay in a restaurant,
for example. ....

22 You're in one now. ....

23 A group of (office) workers. ....

24 Swallowed with water; kind of medicine. ....

Now try and add a few Double Trivia clues of your own.

Give them to your friend to find the answers!

© Cambridge University Press 2000

Suggested words for spelling tests

The lists include words from the '-ck' spelling pattern.

1 *Beginners*

class	chess	ball	bus	fill
has	kick	pass	doll	dress

2 *Intermediate*

gas	staff	brick	plus	until
grass	puff	off	stack	glasses
this	travel	drill	dresses	smaller

3 *Advanced*

seagull	impress	windmill	congress	depressed
unless	swelling	happiness	inkwell	stiffness
cliff	chicken	crackers	misspell	stuffed

Answers

A1

1 shell   2 kiss   3 smell   4 pass   5 glass   6 boss   7 ball   8 grass
9 bell   10 pill   11 small   12 chess   13 bull   14 dress   15 class
16 wall

A2

1 shell   2 Choose from: kiss, pass, glass, boss, grass, dress, class
3 boss   4 Choose from: kiss, smell, pass, boss, dress
5 bell   6 dress   7 small   8 grass   9 class   10 chess

B1

1 staff   2 dress   3 hill   4 well   5 grass   6 glass   7 sell   8 wall
9 hell   10 puff   11 class   12 shell   13 chess   14 kiss   15 bell
16 ass   17 spill   18 cliff   19 doll   20 ball

B3

1 cliff   2 glass   3 kiss   4 drill   5 stuff   6 ill   7 ball   8 cross
9 chess   10 boss   11 less   12 press   13 quill   14 cuff   15 off
16 full   17 mill   18 grass   19 smell   20 gull   21 bill   22 class
23 staff   24 pill

3.2 '-dge'

Lesson plan

Note:

1 In this lesson we will look at the sound /dʒ/ when it is spelled
'-dge'. This spelling pattern is found at the end of single-syllable words
and is preceded by a single vowel letter. You might like to tell students
that the letter 'j' is never found at the end of an English word.

2 Words that end in '-ge' are preceded by a consonant or a long
vowel sound, as in *cage* or *range*. This spelling pattern will be covered
thoroughly in a later unit, but '-ge' words are used in this lesson as a
comparison.

3 Because '-dge' words are usually found in words more suitable to
the intermediate and advanced levels, this spelling pattern should only
be introduced to students at these levels.

1 ELICIT: Ask students to suggest single-syllable words that have a short vowel sound and end with the sound /dʒ/ as in *judge*. Write them on the board. Acceptable examples:

   judge   bridge   fridge   ledge   lodge

2 ASK: What spelling pattern can we deduce from this? Note students' suggestions.

3 WRITE ON THE BOARD:

> We write '-dge' at the end of a single-syllable word, preceded by one vowel letter.
>
> -adge   -edge   -idge   -odge   -udge

4 REMIND AND REVIEW: At this point you might quickly review the other spelling phenomena that are similar to this pattern ('-ck', '-ss', '-ll', '-ff', and '-zz').

Common exceptions

The following common words are exceptions because they have more than one syllable, yet are still spelled with '-dge':

badger   midget   gadget   ledger   fidget

You might suggest that students add this to their notebooks, with examples and a separate note for exceptions.

Warm-up practice of '-dge' spelling pattern

The purpose of these listening exercises is to reinforce the aural differentiation between short and long vowel sounds which precede the sound /dʒ/.

* Intermediate
All words in this activity end in /dʒ/: '-dge' or '-ge'.
   On the board, write the following beginnings of words, which the students can copy into their notebooks:

1 pa ___	2 e ___	3 wa ___	4 bri ___	5 fu ___
6 ca ___	7 he ___	8 villa ___	9 fri ___	10 ju ___

Now read out the following words and tell the students to write the endings.

1 **page**	2 **edge**	3 **wage**	4 **bridge**	5 **fudge**
6 **cage**	7 **hedge**	8 **village**	9 **fridge**	10 **judge**

* *Advanced*
In this activity, the words end in both the sound /dʒ/ (spelled either '-dge' or '-ge') and in the sound /g/, spelled 'g'. After writing out the following word pairs on the board, call out one word from each pair and let the students write the word they hear.

1 **jug – judge**	2 **stag – stage**	3 **edge – age**
4 **bug – budge**	5 **log – lodge**	6 **cadge – cage**
7 **hug – huge**	8 **bag – badge**	9 **leg – ledge**
10 **rig – ridge**		

Alternatively, you can read both pairs of words, but sometimes changing the order, i.e. read **judge jug**. The students can now write both words in the order that they hear them.

A Intermediate

1 Board game

This is a game for two to four players. You need a die and counters or buttons. Make copies of the game and stick them onto cardboard. Each player throws the die. The highest throw goes first. Players read the instructions written in some of the squares and follow them accordingly. The winner is the player who reaches the end first and can recall five of the '-dge' words used in the game.

START	1	2	3
	You have won a free ticket to the Dodgers' baseball game. Go now!		Sit on the HEDGE for one turn.
4 You like FUDGE – don't wait: eat!	5	6 Go for a vacation in the LODGE.	7
8	9	10	11
12	13	14	15 Draw a BADGE before your next turn.
16	17	18 Go and stand on the BRIDGE.	19
20	21	22	23 The FRIDGE door is open – go back and shut it.
24	25	26 Go back to the JUDGE to pay a fine.	27
28 Take a ride on the SLEDGE.	29	30	31
32	33	34 Go and sit on the LEDGE.	Congratulations! You've reached **THE END**

2 Delete and complete

Delete the extra letter from each word. Write the letter you have deleted in the space following the word. Now rearrange these letters to spell out another word for 'small person'.

1 J U D G E M M E N T ___

2 B U D G E T T ___

3 V I L L A D G E ___

4 B R I D I G E ___

5 L O E D G E ___

6 B A G D G E ___

B Advanced

1 Which one?

There is a choice of two answers for each Trivia question. Test your general knowledge by circling what you think is the correct answer. If the questions are too difficult, you or your teacher can compose other questions, where '-dge' or '-ge' words are either in the question or in the answer.

1 Who was the famous actress: **Bridget Bardot** or **Bridget Nelson?**

2 Which city has a famous bridge: **New York** or **San Francisco?**

3 Who was Sylvester Stallone's film judge: **Judge Fred** or **Judge Dred?**

4 Which city do the Dodgers play for: **Los Angeles** or **Atlanta?**

5 Which one is an animal: **a badge** or **a badger?**

6 Which can you ride in the snow: **a sledge** or **a smudge?**

7 Which one is a wooden cabin: **a dredge** or **a lodge?**

8 Which one could you teach to talk: **a badger** or **a budgie?**

9 Which one is for keeping food cold: **a fridge** or **a fidget?**

10 Where might you find a hedge: in **a garden** or in **a house?**

Suggested words for spelling test

The lists include '-ss' and '-ll' words.

1 *Intermediate*

age	chess	small	judge	cliff
kiss	fridge	large	bell	dress
badger	boss	falling	edge	bridge

2 *Advanced*

abridge	village	stuffing	judgement	package
knowledge	passage	budget	badger	dislodge
confess	calling	midget	college	compress

Answers

A2

1 M   2 T   3 D   4 I   5 E   6 G = MIDGET

B1

1 Bridget Bardot   2 San Francisco   3 Judge Dred   4 Los Angeles
5 badger   6 sledge   7 lodge   8 budgie   9 fridge   10 a garden

3.3 '-tch'

Lesson plan

Note:
1 In this lesson we will study the sound /tʃ/ when it is spelled '-tch'. This spelling pattern is found at the end of a single-syllable word and is preceded by one vowel letter.

2 Words that end in '-ch' are preceded by a consonant, as in *lunch*. Words that follow the '-ch' spelling pattern are included in the exercises.

3 Because '-tch' words are usually found in words more suitable to the intermediate and advanced levels, this spelling pattern should only be introduced to students at these levels.

1 ELICIT: Ask students to suggest one-syllable one-vowel letter words that end with the sound /tʃ/ as in *witch*. Acceptable examples:

witch   catch   sketch   Scotch   Dutch

2 ASK: What spelling pattern can we deduce from this? Note the students' suggestions.

3 WRITE ON THE BOARD:

> We write '-tch' at the end of a single-syllable word, preceded by one vowel letter.
>
> -atch   -etch   -itch   -otch   -utch

Common exceptions

You might want to point out that the spelling of the words **such, much, which, rich** do not follow the pattern.

Note:
Now might be a good time to remind the students that we add '-es' to the plurals and third person singular in the Present Simple of '-tch' and '-ch' words, as in **watch – watches** and **lunch – lunches**.

You might suggest that students add this to their notebooks, with examples and a separate note for exceptions.

Warm-up practice of '-tch' spelling pattern

This listening exercise is used not only to strengthen the auditory and visual memory of '-tch' words through repetition but also encourages the students to continue improving short vowel sound recognition.

* Intermediate
Instruct the students to write the numbers one to ten in a column in their notebook. Explain to them that each word they are about to hear ends in '-tch'. As you read out the following words, students must try to write them correctly.

**crutch   stitch   match   patch   Dutch   witch   etch
hutch   ditch   clutch**

* Advanced

This exercise includes '-tch' and '-ch' words. Instruct the students to write the numbers one to ten in a column in their notebook. Explain to them that the words they are about to hear end either in '-tch' or '-ch'. As you read out the following words, students must try to write them correctly.

**much   crutch   ditch   bunch   etch   stitch   such
touch   launch   match**

An alternative method would be to let the students work in pairs, with each student within the pair having a different list of words. Students take turns reading out the words to each other and writing down what they hear.

A Intermediate

1 Tongue twister

Write the following tongue twister sentence on the board and let the students try to say it as quickly as possible.

**If three witches watched three watches,
which witch watched which watch?**

You could now erase the '-tch' and '-ch' words from the sentence and have the students try to reproduce as much of the sentence as they can in their notebooks.

2 Picture the word

a. Look at each word on the left. Find two words and pictures which rhyme with it on each row.

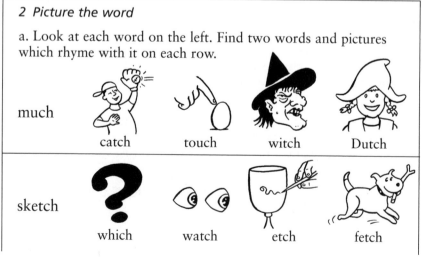

much   catch   touch   witch   Dutch

sketch   which   watch   etch   fetch

© Cambridge University Press 2000

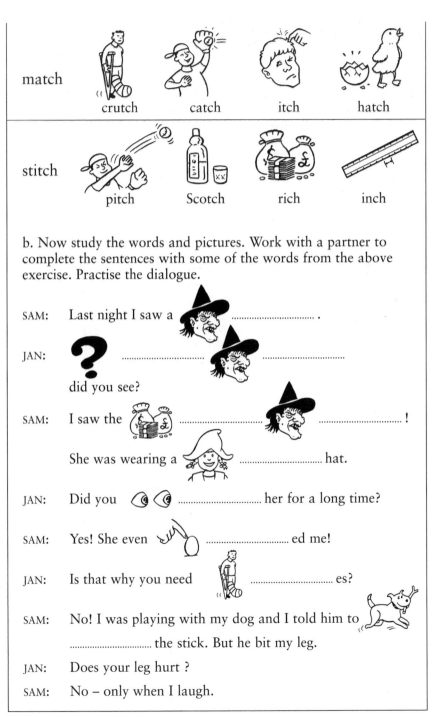

match				
	crutch	catch	itch	hatch

stitch				
	pitch	Scotch	rich	inch

b. Now study the words and pictures. Work with a partner to complete the sentences with some of the words from the above exercise. Practise the dialogue.

SAM: Last night I saw a ....

JAN: .... did you see?

SAM: I saw the .... ! She was wearing a .... hat.

JAN: Did you .... her for a long time?

SAM: Yes! She even .... ed me!

JAN: Is that why you need .... es?

SAM: No! I was playing with my dog and I told him to .... the stick. But he bit my leg.

JAN: Does your leg hurt ?

SAM: No – only when I laugh.

© Cambridge University Press 2000

B Advanced

1 Spell well

a. Form words by adding 'ch' or 'tch' to the end of these letter clusters. Remember: 'ch' follows a consonant or long vowel sound and 'tch' follows a short vowel sound.

1 ca _____	6 scra _____	11 fe _____
2 rea _____	7 clu _____	12 pea _____
3 sti _____	8 bi _____	13 ma _____
4 in _____	9 ben _____	14 bea _____
5 lun _____	10 pun _____	15 ki _____ en

b. Look carefully at the spelling of the words. Working with a partner, take turns testing each other's spelling of the words on the list.

c. Still working with a partner, make up a short story, using as many words from the list as possible. Try to incorporate suffixes such as '-ing', '-ed', '-es'. In groups, share your stories.

2 Phrase it

Use a dictionary to help you find a suitable ending in Column B for the words and phrases in Column A.

Column A	Column B
1 hatch	watchers
2 patchwork	hutch
3 thatched	an egg
4 bird	pitch
5 sketch a	picture
6 he ditched	roof
7 scratch when	quilt
8 'A stitch in time ...'	it itches
9 black as ...	saves nine
10 a rabbit	the car

Suggested words for spelling test

The lists include '-ch' words.

1 *Intermediate*

ranch	catch	witch	Dutch	lunch
which	watch	such	patch	teach
Scotch	stitch	match	inch	touch

2 *Advanced*

ranchers	snatch	sketch	rich	watch
etch	coach	ditch	patches	preach
arch	stitches	matchmaker	itched	pinching

Answers

A2a

touch, Dutch
etch, fetch
catch, hatch
pitch, rich

A2b

SAM: Last night I saw a *witch*.

JAN: *Which witch* did you see?

SAM: I saw the *rich witch*! She was wearing a *Dutch* hat.

JAN: Did you *watch* her for a long time?

SAM: Yes! She even *touched* me!

JAN: Is that why you need *crutches*?

SAM: No! I was playing with my dog and I told him to *fetch* the stick. But he bit my leg.

JAN: Does your leg hurt ?

SAM: No – only when I laugh.

Single vowel followers

B1a

1 catch   2 reach   3 stitch   4 inch   5 lunch   6 scratch
7 clutch   8 bitch   9 bench   10 punch   11 fetch   12 peach
13 match   14 beach   15 kitchen

B2

1 hatch an egg

2 patchwork quilt

3 thatched roof

4 bird watchers

5 sketch a picture

6 he ditched the car

7 scratch when it itches

8 'A stitch in time saves nine.'

9 black as pitch

10 a rabbit hutch

4   The sound 'i' (/aɪ/)

4.1 'i-e'

Lesson plan

This unit deals with the three different spelling patterns that have the sound /aɪ/ as in *time*, *sky* and *flight*. The first lesson in this unit will concentrate on one-syllable words that have the letter 'i' in the middle and are followed by one consonant and then an 'e'. This follows what is commonly known as the Magic – or Silent – 'E' pattern, which is the most common way of spelling the long /aɪ/ sound when it is heard in the middle of a one-syllable word.

1 ELICIT: Ask students to suggest one-syllable words that have the /aɪ/ sound in the middle and are followed by the sound of a single consonant. Write the words on the board. Possible examples:

   bike   time   ride   nice   white   five

   Note:
   If words such as **light** or **right** are suggested, it's better to write them separately on the board, since they are words that do not follow this spelling pattern but will be introduced later.

2 ASK: What spelling pattern can we deduce from this? Note students' suggestions.

3 WRITE ON THE BOARD:

> When we hear 'i' saying its name in the middle of a
> one-syllable word followed by a single consonant
> sound, our first choice is to write
>
> i-e.

Adding a suffix

You might like to point out that when adding a suffix that begins with a vowel ('-ed', '-en', '-ing', etc.) to an 'i-e' word, then you must drop the 'e' from the base word, for example,

write + ing = writing   ripe + en = ripen   smile + ed = smiled

You might suggest that students add both the spelling pattern and the suffix rule to their notebooks.

Warm-up practice of 'i-e' spelling pattern

* *Beginners and intermediate*

1 The purpose of this listening exercise is to strengthen the visual-aural perception of the long vowel /aɪ/ sound.

    The table below can be written on the board for the students to copy into their notebooks, and then to fill in the missing consonants as you read out the following words:

fine   mile   kite   wine   size   like   fire   dive   side   life

1	i	e
2	i	e
3	i	e
4	i	e
5	i	e
6	i	e
7	i	e
8	i	e
9	i	e
10	i	e

2 This listening exercise practises the differentiation between the short /ɪ/ as in *sit* and long /aɪ/ as in *time*.

    Write the following words on the board and as you read one word from each pair, students write the word they have heard. An additional challenge can be added by reading out the words at random.

bite – bit   pin – pine   Sid – side   Tim – time   pill – pile
miss – mice   shine – shin   quit – quite   lick – like   pipe – pip

* *Advanced*
Read out the following pairs of words and ask the students to write
both words in the order they hear them.

    pin – pine   quite – quit   fill – file   Mick – Mike   wit – white
    lick – like   dim – dime   spine – spin   pile – pill   while – will

For additional practice, students can work in pairs, reading out five to
six words for their partner to write down before exchanging roles.

A Beginners

1 Picture word cross

Below are pictures of words that follow the 'i-e' spelling pattern.
Write the names of the pictures in the Word Cross squares
according to their numbers. Do as many as you can in less
than five minutes.

2 All 'i-e'

Solve the clues on the left and write the words in the boxes on the same line. Do at least eight.

		i		e
1 A number, half of ten.		i		e
2 A woman at her wedding.		i		e
3 It has two wheels.		i		e
4 A colour.		i		e
5 Not hate.		i		e
6 A happy face.		i		e
7 The clock tells us this.		i		e
8 A reward.		i		e
9 Plural of 'mouse'.		i		e
10 The police fight this.		i		e
11 Belongs to me.		i		e

B Intermediate

1 Letter leads

Solve the clues and write the answers on the lines, one letter on each line. The letter in the circle will always be the first letter of the next word. Do as many as you can in five minutes.

1 The river of Egypt.   N   I (L) E

2 A citrus fruit.   L ___ ( ) ___

3 A measure of distance.   ___ ___ ( ) ___

4 Not death, but …   — — ◯ —

5 It's very hot.   — — ◯ —

6 Ready to eat, like fruit.   — — ◯ —

7 When proud you have this.   — — — ◯ —

8 'Lead' a car.   — — — ◯ —

9 Where grapes grow.   — — ◯ —

10 Pleasant.   — — ◯ —

11 *… and Punishment*   — — — ◯ —

12 Short for 'microphone'.   — — ◯ —

13 A sharp cutting tool.   — — — ◯ —

14 Like a sunny day.   — — ◯ —

---

2 Up, down, left and right

a. The answers to the clues are all in the grid. You must start at the letter given (in the grid it will have a dot in the corner of its square) and then move one square in any direction – up, down, left or right – changing direction when necessary, in order to discover the words.

H	E	M	I	K	B	D	F
I	D	W	T	E	E	R	I
E	L	I	N	I	U	Q	V
Z	I	M	E	T	E	N	E
P	R	S	J	C	L	I	K

Start at P:
A reward =   P R I Z E

Start at D:
Go by car =   ___ ___ ___ ___ ___

Start at H:
Take cover – don't be found =   ___ ___ ___ ___

Start at N:
River in Egypt =   ___ ___ ___ ___

Start at S:
A happy face has this =   ___ ___ ___ ___ ___

Start at T:
What a clock tells you =   ___ ___ ___ ___

Start at K:
Fly this on a windy day =   ___ ___ ___ ___

Start at W:
Drink make from grapes =   ___ ___ ___ ___

Start at L:
Almost love =   ___ ___ ___ ___

Start at Q:
Very; almost =   ___ ___ ___ ___ ___

Start at F:
'Ready, aim and ...' =   ___ ___ ___ ___

b. Use some of the words you have found to complete these sentences.

1 I want to take your photo, so .... please!

2 With the wind there is today, we can fly our ....

3 Always be careful when you light a ....

4 Did you know that .... is made from grapes?

5 I won a .... in the contest when I came in second.

6 What's the .... ? I think it must be after seven o'clock.

C Advanced

1 Short and long

On the left of each sentence are two words: one with a short 'i' sound, as in *sit* and one with a long 'i' sound as in *time*. Complete the sentences, using each of the two words in the correct spaces. Use your dictionary to help you. Try to do as many as you can.

1 **rid – ride**   Get .... of your gum when you .... on the bus.

2 **pin – pine**   I found a small .... under the .... tree.

3 **spit – spite**   In .... of himself, he had to .... out the truth.

4 **slim – slime**   There was a .... trail of .... left by the snail.

5 **trip – tripe**   If you want to buy .... take a .... to the shop.

6 **fin – fine**   That fish has a .... !

7 **strip – stripe**   You can't .... the ....s from a zebra's
back.

8 **din – dine**   Don't .... in that restaurant: the .... is
so loud!

9 **still – stile**   He stood .... on the .... before going
into the field.

10 **win – wine**   I'll give you a bottle of .... if you ....
the race.

---

2 Word match

Work in pairs and match the words from the box to the meanings
below. Use your dictionary to help you. Try to do as many as you
can.

> squire   twice   stride   knife
>
>   scribe   crime   shrine
> tribe
>
>   thrice   bride   stripe
>   sprite
>
> prize   chive   pride

1   T W I C E   Two times.

2   __ __ __ __ __ __   One of 13 on the American flag.

3   __ __ __ __ __   Looks like grass, tastes like
onion.

4 __ __ __ __ __ __   A type of fairy.

5 __ __ __ __ __   An illegal act.

6 __ __ __ __ __ __   A long step.

7 __ __ __ __ __   The woman on her wedding day.

8 __ __ __ __ __ __   Three times.

9 __ __ __ __ __   A clan or group of people.

10 __ __ __ __ __ __   A writer of documents.

11 __ __ __ __ __   A sharp cutting tool.

12 __ __ __ __ __ __   A place of worship.

13 __ __ __ __ __   A reward.

14 __ __ __ __ __ __   A gentleman landowner, once.

15 __ __ __ __ __   A good feeling, after success.

3 Building blocks

Complete the building blocks by solving the clues. Use the same letters plus one more each time as you go down to the middle (seven-letter) word. Rearrange the letters each time to form your new words. Remove one letter and rearrange the remaining letters as you go down from the middle word to the bottom. The first word (which has been done for you) is the same as the last.

The sound 'i' (/aɪ/)

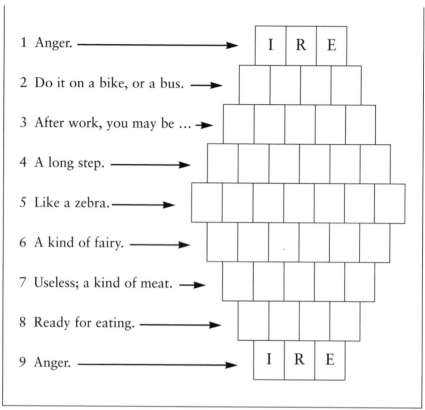

1 Anger. ⟶   I   R   E

2 Do it on a bike, or a bus. ⟶

3 After work, you may be ... ⟶

4 A long step. ⟶

5 Like a zebra. ⟶

6 A kind of fairy. ⟶

7 Useless; a kind of meat. ⟶

8 Ready for eating. ⟶

9 Anger. ⟶   I   R   E

Suggested words for spelling test

1 *Beginners*
These words follow the 'i-e' spelling pattern only.

smile	ride	write	bike	prize
fire	nice	fine	drive	life

2 *Intermediate*
These words contain the sound /ɪ/ as in *sit* and /aɪ/ as in *time*.
Some of the /ɪ/ words follow spelling patterns learnt in Units 2 and 3.

kit	smiling	crime	pride	trick
bill	kite	quite	rich	bridge
quit	bride	wife	vine	writing

3 *Advanced*

These words contain the sound /ɪ/ as in *sit* and /aɪ/ as in *time*. Some of the /ɪ/ words follow spelling patterns learnt in Units 2 and 3. In addition there are compound words and words with affixes.

sunrise	abridge	besides	hitch-hike	inspiring
likely	admire	profile	judgement	define
ripen	sliding	strike	hiding	twice

Answers

A1

1 pipe   2 five   3 fire   4 mice   5 dive   6 bike   7 kite   8 wine
9 time   10 bite   11 nine   12 hide

A2

1 five   2 bride   3 bike   4 white   5 like   6 smile   7 time   8 prize
9 mice   10 crime   11 mine

B1

1 Nile   2 lime   3 mile   4 life   5 fire   6 ripe   7 pride   8 drive
9 vine   10 nice   11 crime   12 mike   13 knife   14 fine

B2a

prize   drive   hide   Nile   smile   time   kite   wine   like   quite
fire

B2b

smile   kite   fire   wine   prize   time

C1

1 Get **rid** of your gum when you **ride** on the bus.
2 I found a small **pin** under the **pine** tree.
3 In **spite** of himself, he had to **spit** out the truth.
4 There was a **slim** trail of **slime** left by the snail.
5 If you want to buy **tripe** take a **trip** to the shop.
6 That fish has a **fine fin**!
7 You can't **strip** the **stripes** from a zebra's back.
8 Don't **dine** in that restaurant: the **din** is so loud!
9 He stood **still** on the **stile** before going into the field.
10 I'll give you a bottle of **wine** if you **win** the race.

C2

1 twice   2 stripe   3 chive   4 sprite   5 crime   6 stride   7 bride
8 thrice   9 tribe   10 scribe   11 knife   12 shrine   13 prize
14 squire   15 pride

C3

2 ride   3 tired   4 stride   5 striped   6 sprite   7 tripe   8 ripe

4.2 '-y'

Lesson plan

Note:
Although most one-syllable words with the sound /aɪ/ are spelled 'i-e'
as *time*, there are two other common spelling patterns for this sound.
In this lesson we are going to look at the sound /aɪ/ at the end of the
word, which is most commonly spelled '-y' as in *sky*. Since English
words cannot end in the letter 'i', it is replaced with 'y', which then
becomes a vowel. The group of words which have a '-y' ending are
few in number, therefore the following exercises will include both 'i-e'
and '-y' words.

1 ELICIT: Ask students to suggest one-syllable words that have the /aɪ/
   sound at the end. Write the words on the board. Possible examples:

   by   fly   cry   try   why

Common exceptions

If **buy, guy** or **die, tie, lie** or **eye, dye** are suggested, you could write
them separately on the board, since these are words that do not follow
this spelling pattern but have to be learnt globally, as 'sight words'.
   If **high** or **sigh** are suggested, tell the students that this spelling
pattern will be introduced later.

2 ASK: What spelling rule can we deduce from this? Note students'
   suggestions.

3 WRITE ON THE BOARD:

> When we hear 'i' saying its name at the end of a
> word, our first choice is to write
> '-y'.

Adding a suffix

You might like to point out the following:

1 Plurals or third person singular in the Present Simple of words that end in consonant + 'y', change the 'y' to 'i' and add 'es', for example,

try – tries   spy – spies

2 When you need to add 'ed' (for the Simple Past) to words that end in consonant + 'y', change the 'y' to i' and add 'ed', for example,

try – tried   spy – spied

You might suggest that students add both the spelling pattern and the suffix rule to their notebooks, with examples and a separate note for exceptions.

Warm-up practice of '-y' spelling pattern

* Beginners

The purpose of this listening exercise is to strengthen the aural-visual awareness of two spelling patterns which are related to the sound /aɪ/: 'i-e', where it is in the middle of the word and '-y', where the sound /aɪ/ is at the end of the word. Draw the table below on the board, numbering it one to ten. Start by telling the students to copy the table into their notebooks.

	i-e	-y
1		
2		
3		

Read out the following words, explaining that students don't have to write down the word they hear, but only tick the appropriate column.

sky wine try fly kite my mine bite dive cry

* *Intermediate and advanced*
Let your students copy down the table from the previous exercise, then explain that they should write out in full the words that they hear in the appropriate column. Read out the following words:

tribe spy mice why bride prize fry sky while shy

A Beginners

---

1 Where's the logic?

In each sentence, the underlined word does not make sense. Replace it with one of the words from the box to make a logical sentence. Rewrite each sentence with the correct word. Do at least seven.

1 When you are sad you <u>smile</u>. ....

2 I want to <u>play</u> an airplane. ....

3 You drink <u>time</u> in a glass. ....

4 I walked in the rain so I wasn't <u>red</u>. ....

5 If you win the race you will get a <u>tree</u>. ....

6 Tell me <u>white</u> you don't like me? ....

7 The sun is shining in the <u>cat</u>. ....

8 You have to <u>black</u> more, then you will get better. ....

9 My <u>dog</u> has two wheels. ....

10 Don't phone, just <u>eat</u> a letter. ....

---

dry	write	wine	**sky**	drive	**my**	fly
prize	bike	ride	white	time	nine	like
try	**why**	five	**cry**	bite	**by**	

© Cambridge University Press 2000

2 Spot the differences

Pair work. Below are two pictures with ten differences. Cut or fold the photocopy, so that each student in the pair has a different picture.

Working in pairs, without showing each other your picture, find at least seven differences by asking each other questions. When you have finished, work together in order to find more 'i-e' and '-y' words which are illustrated in the pictures.

Picture One

Picture Two

© Cambridge University Press 2000

B Intermediate

1 y to i

Answer the following questions with full sentences. Your answers should contain a word that ends in either '-ies' or '-ied' and is based on a '-y' word. Answer at least five questions.

1 What does a hairdrier do?

....

....

2 What does a man do if he wants to see if a new shirt fits?

....

....

3 What is another word for 'answered'?

....

....

4 What are chipped and fried potatoes called in the USA?

....

....

5 What are secret agents also known as?

....

....

6 What is another name for point-scores in the game of rugby?

....

....

7 What insects are unwanted around food on a hot day?

....

....

8 If someone regretted something small that had happened and couldn't be put right, what could we say that he did?

....

....

2 Tell me 'y'

a. Choose '-y' words from the box that logically complete the sentences below. You can use your dictionary.

fly	shy	try, try	why	cry	sly
				my	spy
sky	by	sty	fry	dry	deny

1 I .... with .... little eye, something beginning with ...

2 Every .... has a wherefore.

3 If at first you don't succeed, ... again.

4 He is as .... as a fox.

5 .... bread at home is better than roast beef abroad.

6 Don't .... over spilt milk.

7 Something that goes wrong may have a .... in the ointment.

8 What a mess! Your room is like a pig............... !

9 New York is full of ....scrapers.

10 'For she's a jolly good fellow, which nobody can .... !'

© Cambridge University Press 2000

b. After the students have successfully completed the exercise, you might enjoy encouraging a class discussion about some of the following:

- Which of the sentences have equivalents in the mother tongue?
- Which sentences, in your opinion, are most relevant to you? Why?
- Which sentence reminds you of a true-life incident?

C *Advanced*

1 *Nouns to '-ify' verbs*

a. There are a number of nouns that can be changed to verbs
by replacing their suffix with the suffix '-ify', for example,
justice – justify. Write the following nouns on the board and ask
students to change them to '-ify' verbs. They do as many as they can in
five minutes, using a dictionary for help. Ask if they can think of any
more '-ify' verbs.

1 identity	⇒ identify	9 certificate	⇒
2 satisfaction	⇒	10 simplicity	⇒
3 terror	⇒	11 dignity	⇒
4 class	⇒	12 significance	⇒
5 purity	⇒	13 beauty	⇒
6 horror	⇒	14 unity	⇒
7 testimony	⇒	15 crucifix	⇒
8 mystery	⇒		

b. Storytelling – an oral activity for the whole class. Firstly, you might
like to discuss with your students topical points of interest that they
consider 'hot issues'. Then explain that this now becomes the
background to a story they are going to take turns telling. Students
contribute to the story by saying a sentence that includes an '-ify'
word.

2 Wordsearch

a. Working in pairs, search for words hidden in this wordsearch that end in '-y'. Write each word you find on the lines below the grid. After five minutes, join up with another pair in order to complete the exercise. There are at least 24 words, going from left to right and from top to bottom.

B	U	T	T	E	R	F	L	Y	Y	A	L	L	Y	E
S	P	E	C	I	F	Y	U	V	T	M	S	O	S	L
Y	W	S	A	M	Z	X	L	C	E	P	A	C	Y	E
Q	Y	T	F	P	J	U	L	Y	R	L	T	C	H	C
Y	M	I	P	L	U	R	A	S	R	I	I	U	O	T
D	E	F	Y	Y	S	T	B	H	I	F	S	P	R	R
E	A	Y	W	A	T	H	Y	L	F	Y	F	Y	R	I
N	M	U	L	T	I	P	L	Y	Y	E	Y	F	I	F
Y	N	O	T	I	F	Y	L	Q	U	A	L	I	F	Y
V	E	R	I	F	Y	S	I	M	P	L	I	F	Y	R

....

....

....

....

b. Working in pairs for two minutes, write down as many words as you can remember without looking at the grid. After the time limit has expired, join with another pair for one more minute to add to your list.

Suggested words for spelling test

1 *Beginners*

These words follow the '-y' and 'i-e' spelling patterns.

cry	smile	July	fly	why
bike	try	drive	my	ride

2 *Intermediate*

These words follow the '-y' and 'i-e' spelling patterns and include suffixes.

wipe	dry	pile	sky	line
cried	quite	flies	nine	shy
strike	firing	spying	twice	dives

3 *Advanced*

while	satisfy	spine	notified	qualify
sly	despite	guy	multiplies	pry
amplify	shyness	identified	trying	eye

Answers

A1

1 cry   2 fly   3 wine   4 dry   5 prize/bike   6 why   7 sky
8 try   9 bike   10 write

A2

The ten differences are:

Picture One	Picture Two
1 The fly is on the bottle.	The fly is in the bottle.
2 The bike is at the bottom of the hill.	The bike is at the top of the hill.
3 There's a large fire in the grill.	There's a small fire in the grill.
4 The woman is smoking a pipe.	The man is smoking a pipe.
5 The bride's five flowers are fresh.	The bride's five flowers are not fresh.
6 The time is nine o'clock.	The time is three o'clock.
7 There are stripes down the hat.	There are stripes on the hat brim.
8 There is a smile on the man's face.	There is a smile on the woman's face.
9 The kite is flying high.	The kite is falling down.
10 There are three mice.	There are two mice.

Other 'i-e' and '-y' words:
pine   time   bride   wine   sky   spy   hide   pie

B1

Students could answer the questions as follows:

1 A hairdrier dries your hair.
2 He tries it on.
3 Another word for 'answered' is 'replied'.
4 Chipped potatoes are called French fries in the USA.
5 Secret agents are also known as spies.
6 Point-scores in the game of rugby are tries.
7 Flies are unwanted insects around food on a hot day.
8 We could say he 'cried over spilt milk'.

B2a

1 spy, my   2 why   3 try, try   4 sly   5 Dry   6 cry   7 fly   8 sty
9 sky   10 deny

C1a

1 identify   2 satisfy   3 terrify   4 classify   5 purify   6 horrify
7 testify   8 mystify   9 certify   10 simplify   11 dignify
12 signify   13 beautify   14 unify   15 crucify

C2a

B	U	T	T	E	R	F	L	Y	Y	A	L	L	Y	E
S	P	E	C	I	F	Y	U	V	T	M	S	O	S	L
Y	W	S	A	M	Z	X	L	C	E	P	A	C	Y	E
Q	Y	T	F	P	J	U	L	Y	R	L	T	C	H	C
Y	M	I	P	L	U	R	A	S	R	I	I	U	O	T
D	E	F	Y	Y	S	T	B	H	I	F	S	P	R	R
E	A	Y	W	A	T	H	Y	L	F	Y	F	Y	R	I
N	M	U	L	T	I	P	L	Y	Y	E	Y	F	I	F
Y	N	O	T	I	F	Y	L	Q	U	A	L	I	F	Y
V	E	R	I	F	Y	S	I	M	P	L	I	F	Y	R

These are some of the words we found hidden in the wordsearch:

ply   thy   fly   butterfly   testify   specify   lullaby   ally   July
justify   electrify   verify   defy   multiply   notify   qualify   horrify
simplify   deny   amplify   imply   occupy   terrify   satisfy

4.3 '-igh'

Lesson plan

Note:

There are relatively few words with this pattern, but it is important to teach since it is another accepted form of spelling the sound /aɪ/. This spelling pattern is most commonly found followed by the letter 't', as in *night*, but also appears as a final vowel sound in the words *sigh*, *thigh* and *high*. You may prefer to teach this pattern only to your intermediate and advanced students. The few 'igh' words that appear in a beginner's vocabulary, such as *light, right, night, fight, high* can be taught globally.

1 ELICIT: Ask students to suggest one-syllable words that have the /aɪ/ sound in the middle and are followed by the letter 't'. Write the words on the board. Possible examples:

   night   light   bright   sight

   Note:

   If **bite, white, kite** etc. are suggested, write them separately on the board, since these are words that do not follow this spelling pattern. They were introduced at the beginning of this unit as part of the 'i-e' spelling pattern, being the first choice for spelling the sound /aɪ/.

2 ASK: What spelling pattern can we deduce from this? Note students' suggestions.

3 WRITE ON THE BOARD:

> When we hear /aɪ/, followed by a 't', our second choice will be to write '-igh'.

You can now introduce the three words that end in '-igh', according to the vocabulary level of the class: *sigh, high, thigh*.

   You might suggest that students add this to their notebooks, with examples.

Warm-up practice of '-igh' spelling pattern

The purpose of this listening activity is to strengthen the awareness that most '-igh' words end with a 't'. Therefore, words that end in the sound /aɪt/ will be spelled '-ight', as in *light* and those that end in /aɪ/ will be spelled 'y', as in *fly*.

Instruct the students that in each sentence that they are going to hear, there is one '-ight' word and one '-y' word. They will hear the sentence twice, after which they should try to write down the two words, in the order they hear them.

Read out the following sentences:

• In the evening there was a *bright sky.*
• What a *fright* – I have just seen the *spy.*
• I have to *try* to study for the test *tonight.*
• *Why* is that *sight* so strange to you?
• You *might* like to *fry* the eggs.
• I am going to *fly* on a morning *flight.*
• *My tights* have a hole in them.

A *Intermediate*

1 *Square the letters*

Write the answers to the definitions below in the squares on the same line. All the words follow the '-igh' spelling pattern. Some letters are already in squares to help you. Do at least five.

1 It is not the day.

2 Women may wear them on their legs.

3 Not low.

4 It isn't wrong.

5 Something seen.

6 It scares you.

7 Not dark – or not heavy.

8 A trip on a plane.

© Cambridge University Press 2000

111

2 Tell me about it

Pair work. Cut or fold your copy of the pictures below, so that each student in the pair has a different picture.

Student A has to describe picture A to Student B using the four '-igh' words written below it. Student B has to draw the picture, asking questions which will help with the drawing.

Now change roles, with Student B describing picture B to Student A. When you have both finished, compare your drawings to the originals. Finally, write one to three sentences on the lines provided that describe your 'new' drawings, using your partner's '-igh' words.

Student A

knight   fright   night
sight

Student B

....

....

....

....

....

....

bright   light   high
right

B Advanced

1 The goodnight game

a. Illustrated in the picture are 11 of the following 15 '-igh' words. Find at least seven and write the number of the word on the picture.

1 flightpath	2 tightfisted	3 lighthouse	4 highway
5 watertight	6 headlight	7 stage-fright	8 eyesight
9 moonlight	10 highlands	11 right-handed	12 highjump
13 tightrope	14 sunlight	15 sigh	

b. Write a story, using the picture and at least seven of the '-igh' words. Then, in groups or pairs, compare stories and find at least five content differences between them.

---

2 Light idioms

a. Find the 'light' words and idiomatic expressions in column B that match the descriptions in column A. Write the answers like this: 1 – g. Try to do as many as you can.

A

1 To understand, finally.

2 When there's still some hope.

3 At dawn.

4 To fall asleep quickly.

5 Go!

6 To weigh hardly anything at all.

7 Stop here! There's danger!

8 To take what doesn't belong to you.

9 It shows ships and boats where land is.

10 It often comes with thunder.

11 The British call this 'a torch'.

12 They're on the front of a car.

13 In astronomy, 5,878,000,000,000 miles!

14 Cigarette smokers may use this.

15 A boxer's weight, maybe.

B

a. Be as light as a feather.

b. Lightning.

c. A red light.

d. A light year.

e. A flashlight.

f. At first light.

g. To see the light.

h. Headlights.

i. A green light.

j. Light at the end of a tunnel.

k. To go out like a light.

l. Lightweight.

m. To be light-fingered.

n. A lighter.

o. A lighthouse.

---

b. You might like to discuss with the class similarities and differences between the expressions in the students' mother tongue, difficulties in translating and examples where certain expressions could be used.

Suggested words for spelling test

The lists include all spelling patterns from this unit.

1 *Intermediate*

why	light	frighten	right	skies
while	night	wise	driver	fly
flight	brighter	sunlight	smiling	tonight

2 *Advanced*

deny	frightening	delighted	sunrise	fries
enlighten	nightclub	shortsighted	flying	qualify
retirement	occupy	tightened	surprising	slight

Answers

A1

1 night 2 tights 3 high 4 right 5 sight 6 fright 7 light
8 flight

B1a

B2a

1g 2j 3f 4k 5i 6a 7c 8m 9o 10b 11e 12h 13d
14n 15l

5   The sound 'a' (/eɪ/)

5.1 'a-e'
Lesson plan

This unit deals with the three different spelling patterns that have the /eɪ/ sound in words such as *bake*, *bay*, *bait*. The first lesson in this unit will concentrate on one-syllable words that have the letter 'a' in the middle and are followed by one consonant and then an 'e'. This pattern follows what is commonly known as 'The Magic – or Silent – E' pattern, which is the most common way of spelling the /eɪ/ sound when it is heard in the middle of a one-syllable word.

1 ELICIT: Ask students to suggest one-syllable words that have the /eɪ/ sound in the middle and are followed by the sound of a single consonant. Write the words on the board. Possible examples:

> **bake   name   late   race   cage   male**

Common exceptions

If **eight, weight, freight, reign, feign, feint, steak** or **break** are suggested, you could write them separately on the board, since these are words that do not follow the spelling pattern and have to be learnt globally as 'sight words'.

If words such as **wait** or **rain** are suggested, write them separately on the board, since they are words that do not follow this spelling pattern but will be introduced later.

2 ASK: What spelling pattern can we deduce from this? Note students' suggestions.

3 WRITE ON THE BOARD:

> When we hear 'a' saying its name in the middle of a
> one-syllable word followed by a single consonant sound,
> our first choice is to write
> 'a-e'.

4 ASK: Do you remember, from the previous unit, what happens when
we add a suffix to words that end in 'i-e'? If the suffix begins with a
vowel (as in '-ing', '-ed', '-en') then you must drop the 'e' from the
base word before adding the suffix. The same rule applies to this
spelling pattern, 'a-e', for example,

   race + 'ing' = racing   name + 'ed' = named;   take + 'en' = taken

You might suggest that students add the spelling pattern, the suffix
rule and relevant exceptions to their notebooks.

Warm-up practice of 'a-e' spelling pattern

* *Beginners*
The purpose of this listening exercise is to strengthen the visual-aural
perception of the /eɪ/ sound.

   You can write the following table on the board for the students to
copy into their notebooks. Then they fill in the missing consonants as
you read out these words:

face   make   late   name   cake   hate   care   take
race   snake

1	a	e
2	a	e
3	a	e
4	a	e
5	a	e
6	a	e
7	a	e
8	a	e
9	a	e
10	a	e

* *Intermediate*

This listening exercise practises the differentiation between the sound /æ/ as in *cat* and the sound /eɪ/ as in *plate*. Write the following words on the board and as you read one word from each pair, students write the word they think they hear.

cane – can   rate – rat   mad – made   pal – pale   bake – back
hate – hat   same – Sam   tap – tape   tack – take   mat – mate

* *Advanced*

Students must differentiate between the sound /æ/ as in *cat* and the sound /eɪ/ as in *plate* in order to spell the words. Previously learnt spelling patterns have been included.

Read out some of the following pairs of words. The students write both words in the order they hear them.

fat – fate   plane – plan   tack – take   van – vane   hate – hat
mass – mace   bale – ball   mad – made   cane – can   Dane – Dan

A Beginners

1 All 'a-e'

Solve the clues on the left and write the words in the boxes on the same line. Do as many as you can.

		a		e
1 What people call me.		a		e
2 To stop the car, press the ...		a		e
3 Not different.		a		e
4 Long, thin and says 'sss'.		a		e
5 Run fast and win the ...		a		e
6 Good to drink – a milk ...		a		e
7 Not love.		a		e
8 Somewhere, some ...		a		e
9 To do.		a		e

© Cambridge University Press 2000

		a		e
10 A fruit used in wine.		a		e
11 Part of the body.		a		e
12 It flies in the air.		a		e
13 Bake it for a birthday.		a		e

2 Time for rhyme

Here are two short exercises, all about 'a-e' rhyming words.

a. Can you think of four words that rhyme with 'brake'?
Write them here!

....

Can you think of four words that rhyme with 'blame'? Write them
here!

....

b. Write an 'a-e' word to complete each rhyme. Some of the words
are on this page.

1 I want to bake

   A chocolate ....

2 Come to the gate

   And don't be ....

3 Sam is my name

   Let's play a ....

4 I saw a snake

   Down by the ....

5 I won first place

   In the running ....

Now make up some more rhymes and share them with a friend.

© Cambridge University Press 2000

B Intermediate

1 Wordsearch

Brainstorm the class for words that follow these endings: '-ace', '-age', '-ate', '-are' and '-ave' and write them on the board. Ask the students to choose 10–15 of the words to make their own wordsearch, as on page 107, or crossword puzzle. Tell students that they should add suitable definitions or illustrations that represent the words in their wordsearch. You might first like to come to an agreement as to which directions will be used. Have the students exchange their work for a friend to solve.

---

2 i over a

a. Solve the clues on the left to discover the minimal pair. Write the letters in the correct boxes that complete the words. Do as many as you can.

1	A kind of tree.		i		
	The glass in a window.		a		e

2	A clock tells the ...		i		
	Not wild.		a		e

3	Longer than a kilometre.		i		
	Opposite of female.		a		e

4	A boy's name.		i		
	To do.		a		e

5	Less than love.		i		
	A body of water.		a		e

© Cambridge University Press 2000

6	Flies in the air.	i		e
	A girl's name.	a		

7	Where there's smoke, there's …	i		e
	Pay this on the bus, for example.	a		

8	Ten cents.	i		e
	Old English word for 'lady'.	a		

9	To eat.	i		e
	Someone from Denmark.	a		

10	It belongs to me.	i		e
	It grows on the neck of a horse.	a		

b. Choose three to five pairs of words from the previous exercise and write sentences using both words of the pair.

C Advanced

1 First and second

Solve the riddles to form the 'a-e' words. When you discover the first word, all you have to do is add a letter to the *beginning* of it in order to form the second word. Do at least seven.

Example:

My first is not early: L A T E .

Add a P and my second is something you eat from:

P L A T E .

1 My first is a narrow country road: __ __ __ __ .
   Add a P and my second is a flying machine:

   P __ __ __ __ .

2 My first is a tool for gathering leaves: __ __ __ __ .
   Add a B and my second is a 'stopper' on a car or bike:

   B __ __ __ __ .

3 My first is a running competition: __ __ __ __ .
   Add a T and my second is a small amount: T __ __ __ __ .

4 My first is a rabbit-like animal: __ __ __ __ .
   Add an S and my second means 'to divide': S __ __ __ __ .

5 My first is a holey material: __ __ __ __ .
   Add a P and my second means 'to put': P __ __ __ __ .

6 My first is a stride or a long step: __ __ __ __ .
   Add an S and my second is a lot of room: S __ __ __ __ .

7 My first is a story: __ __ __ __ .
   Add an S and my second is not fresh: S __ __ __ __ .

8 My first is disabled or weak: __ __ __ __ .
   Add a B and my second is guilt: B __ __ __ __ .

9 My first is to look after: __ __ __ __ .

Add an S and my second is to frighten: S __ __ __ __ .

10 My first is to burn down: __ __ __ __ .

Add a G and my second is to scratch or scrape:

G __ __ __ __ .

---

2 Circle pairs

a. When you use all the letters in the circles, you will find two or three pairs of 'a-e' words. Can you find them? Make sure that you use all the letters, but each letter only once. Try to do as many as you can.

1

H A
A T R
M E E

....

....

....

2

K C
B A E
E R
A

....

....

....

3

W E
A K E
A
S N
V

....

....

....

4

T E
A F K
M E
A

....

....

....

5

L T
K A E
E A
C

....

....

....

6

A A
G D E
M E
T

....

....

....

© Cambridge University Press 2000

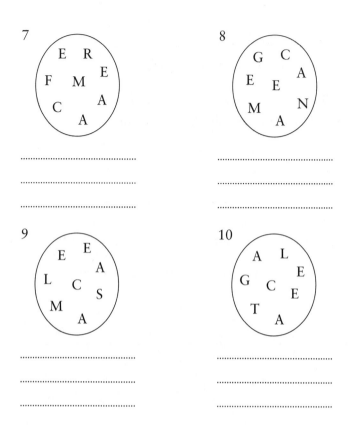

7

E R
F M E
C A
A

8

G C
E E A
M N
A

9

E E
E A
L C S
M A

10

A L
G E
C E
T A

b. Make up strange or funny headlines using the answers from the previous exercise, for example, The Case Of The Baked Snake.

c. In groups, choose one of the headlines and write a short article or story.

Suggested words for spelling test

1 *Beginners*
These words follow the 'a-e' spelling pattern only.

made	face	came	cake	date
grape	page	game	race	take

2 *Intermediate*
These words all follow the 'a-e' spelling pattern, but in addition some have prefixes and suffixes.

snake	raced	making	mistake	blamed
tamer	careful	prepare	daring	naming
erase	lately	bravest	taken	shaded

3 *Advanced*
The words all follow the 'a-e' spelling pattern but some compound words also include previous spelling patterns, prefixes and suffixes.

grateful	undertake	framework	hesitate	shaving
chased	naked	handshake	stagefright	baseline
awareness	fireplace	imitated	careless	pacemaker

Answers

A1

1 name 2 brake 3 same 4 snake 5 race 6 shake 7 hate
8 place 9 make 10 grape 11 face 12 plane 13 cake

A2a

Possible words are:
bake cake lake snake fake shake wake awake stake
flake
lame tame came game name fame flame same dame
shame

A2b

1 cake 2 late 3 game 4 lake 5 race

B2a

1 pine, pane 2 time, tame 3 mile, male 4 Mike, make
5 like, lake 6 kite, Kate 7 fire, fare 8 dime, dame
9 dine, Dane 10 mine, mane

C1

1 lane – plane   2 rake – brake   3 race – trace   4 hare – share
5 lace – place   6 pace – space   7 tale – stale   8 lame – blame
9 care – scare   10 raze – graze

C2a

We found the following words – there may be other variations.

Circle 1: hate – mare;   tame (or mate) – hare
Circle 2: bare – cake;   bake – race (or care)
Circle 3: vane – wakes;   snake – wave
Circle 4: take – fame;   fake – mate (or tame)
Circle 5: lace – take;   cake – tale (or late)
Circle 6: game – date;   gate – dame (or made)
Circle 7: face – mare;   fame – race (or care);   fare – came (or mace)
Circle 8: cane – game;   cage – mane (or name)
Circle 9: case – male (or lame);   same – lace;   mace – sale
Circle 10: gate – lace;   cage – late (or tale)

5.2 '-ay'

Lesson plan

Note:
Although most one-syllable words with the sound /eɪ/ are spelled 'a-e',
there are two other patterns which are common. In this lesson we are
going to look at the sound /eɪ/ at the end of the word, which is most
commonly spelled '-ay' as in *play*. Since English words cannot end in
the letter 'a', the letter 'y' is added to make a vowel diphthong. The
group of words which have an '-ay' ending are few in number,
therefore some of the exercises in this part of the unit will include
both 'a-e' and '-ay' words.

1 ELICIT: Ask students to suggest one-syllable words that have the /eɪ/
   sound at the end. Write the words on the board. Possible examples:

   say   may   play   tray   way

Common exceptions

If **they, grey** (as an alternative to 'gray'), **prey, hey, survey, weigh** or **sleigh** are suggested, write them separately on the board, since they do not follow the spelling pattern but have to be learned globally, as 'sight words'.

2 ASK: What spelling pattern can we deduce from this? Note students' suggestions.

3 WRITE ON THE BOARD:

> When we hear 'a' saying its name at the end
> of a word, our first choice is to write
> '-ay'.

You might suggest that the students copy the spelling pattern and the exceptions into their notebooks.

Warm-up practice of '-ay' spelling pattern

* Beginners

The purpose of this listening exercise is to strengthen the aural-visual awareness of two spelling patterns which are related to the /eɪ/ sound: 'a-e' as in *cake*, and '-ay' as in *day*.

Write this table up on the board for the students to copy into their notebooks. Read out one word from each pair and let the students circle the word they think they heard.

	a-e	-ay
1	make	May
2	plane	play
3	save	say
4	date	day
5	whale	way
6	grade	gray
7	page	pay

The sound 'a' (/eɪ/)

* *Intermediate*
Let the students copy the following grid into their notebooks,
numbering from one to seven:

	a-e	-ay
1		
2		
3		

Using the words from the beginners' exercise, read out one word from
each pair and have the students write it in the appropriate column.

* *Advanced*
This listening exercise practises four spelling patterns: 'i-e', '-y', 'a-e'
and '-ay'. Write this grid on the board and ask the students to copy it
into their notebooks:

	i-e	-y	a-e	-ay
1				
2				
3				
4				
5				

Read out two or three words from each spelling pattern. Students
should write the words they hear in the appropriate column of their
grid.

fire   fry   fare   Fay
mine   my   mane   may
bike   by   bake   bay
wine   why   wane   way
pile   ply   pale   play

A Beginners

1 Way to go!

a. Complete the following sentences by choosing two out of the three words. Do as many as you can.

1 Please .... when you will ....   (**pay, gray, say**)

2 We ran .... on the .... to school.   (**way, away, stay**)

3 .... is Monday so yesterday was ....
(**Wednesday, Sunday, Today**)

4 Mark and Jo wanted to .... football and not .... at
school.   (**subway, stay, play**)

5 We went to France for our .... last ....
(**holiday, May, yesterday**)

b. Ten of the '-ay' words from the previous exercise are hidden in this wordsearch. How many can you find? Search from left to right and from top to bottom. Write the words you find on the lines next to the grid.

Y	E	S	T	E	R	D	A	Y
G	Y	S	U	B	W	A	Y	T
R	Y	T	Y	A	Y	P	A	O
A	W	A	Y	Y	M	A	Y	D
Y	A	Y	P	L	A	Y	Y	A
W	E	D	N	E	S	D	A	Y

....
....
....
....
....
....
....
....

B *Intermediate*

1 *Play with syllables*

Form the words to fit the definitions by putting together syllables from the box. You use each syllable only once, so it's a good idea to cross them off as you use them. Write each letter on a dash beside the definitions. The number of syllables you need for each word is given. Do as many as you can.

1 At a distance (3)	f a r /a /w a y
2 For ever and ever (2)	_ _ / _ _ _ _
3 A city in India (2)	_ _ _ / _ _ _
4 A pile of dry grass (2)	_ _ _ / _ _ _ _ _
5 Muslim day of rest (2)	_ _ _ / _ _ _
6 To rot (2)	_ _ / _ _ _
7 To put off (2)	_ _ / _ _ _
8 A writing assignment (2)	_ _ / _ _ _
9 Not during the night (2)	_ _ _ / _ _ _ _
10 Not serious; jokes a lot (2)	_ _ _ _ / _ _ _
11 Noon (2)	_ _ _ / _ _ _
12 Hip – hip – ...! (2)	_ _ _ / _ _ _
13 The day before today (3)	_ _ _ / _ _ _ _ / _ _ _
14 A child who leaves home (3)	_ _ _ / _ / _ _ _
15 A car path to the house (2)	_ _ _ _ _ / _ _ _

~~a~~	a	al	bay	Bom	cay	day	day day day
de	de	drive	es	~~far~~	ful	hay	hur lay
mid	play	ray	run	Fri	say	stack	ter
time	way	~~way~~	way	ways	yes		

2 Bingo

Brainstorm the class for at least 20 words that follow the two spelling patterns: 'a-e' and '-ay'. Write their suggestions on the board. Also on the board, draw the following Bingo card for them to copy into their notebooks.

Bingo!

Students choose words from the board to fill up their cards. In order to increase class participation, you might like to have the students take turns calling out words from the board which are *not* on their card. If the other students hear a word that is on their card, they cover it up or cross it off. As the teacher, you can decide on the method of winning: either the first to complete one row, one column, one diagonal or the whole card. The winner calls out 'Bingo!' and has to read out the words that form the winning card.

C Advanced

1 Boxing words

On the right are fragmented '-ay' words which can be completed by first reading the clues then choosing, each time, the correct two boxes from those on the left. Cross off the boxes as you go, as each box can only be used once. Do as many as you can.

© Cambridge University Press 2000

The sound 'a' (/eɪ/)

Clues
1. Not serious; lively and happy.
2. Remain too long.
3. Like a profile, not from the front.
4. Toy.
5. One of the days of the week.
6. Pile of dry grass, found on farms.
7. Return money or a favour.
8. The day before today.
9. Not a professional.
10. Small dishes for cigarette stubs.

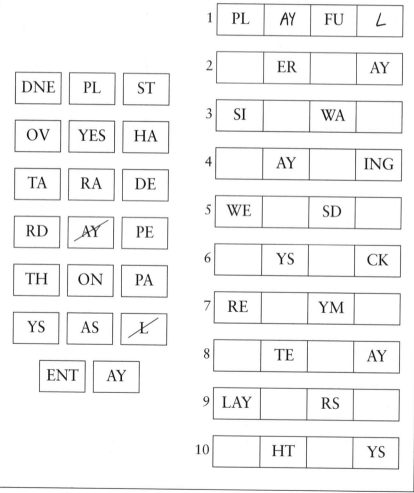

	DNE	PL	ST
TA	RA	DE	
RD	A̶Y̶	PE	
TH	ON	PA	
YS	AS	L̶	
	ENT	AY	

1	PL	AY	FU	L
2		ER		AY
3	SI		WA	
4		AY		ING
5	WE		SD	
6		YS		CK
7	RE		YM	
8		TE		AY
9	LAY		RS	
10		HT		YS

2 Word scramble

This is a game for two to four players working together on the same board. Each player has a different coloured pen. Taking turns, each player writes an '-ay' or 'a-e' word on the board. The first word must cover the START square. Each word that is added must connect to a word that is already on the board, in crossword fashion. (No diagonals allowed.) Players may also add suffixes and prefixes to existing words. Score one point for each letter and then add bonus points if a word falls on a shaded square (see below).

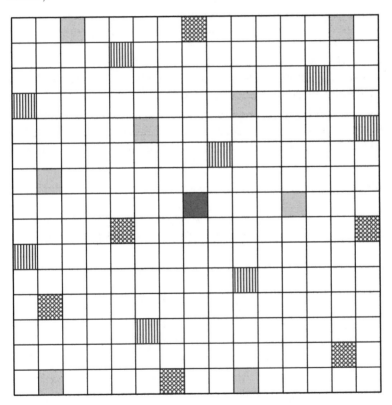

START AT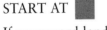

If your word lands on ▨ double the word score.

If your word lands on ▥ triple the word score.

If your word lands on ▨ give yourself ten more points.

Suggested words for spelling test

1 *Beginners*
   These words follow only the '-ay' spelling pattern.

may	play	say	tray	way
gray	holiday	Sunday	stay	Friday

2 *Intermediate*
   These words follow the '-ay' and 'a-e' spelling patterns + affixes + the irregular word 'they'.

playmate	delay	tape	hateful	they
shaving	yesterday	replay	subway	date
raced	mistake	Monday	daring	stage

3 *Advanced*
   These words follow the '-ay' and 'a-e' spelling patterns + affixes + the irregular words 'survey' and 'weigh'.

relay	delayed	gratefully	carelessness	highway
weigh	hesitating	survey	betray	daylight
straying	namely	wages	hated	always

Answers

A1a

1 say, pay   2 away, way   3 Today, Wednesday   4 play, stay
5 holiday, May

A1b

Y	E	S	T	E	R	D	A	Y
G	Y	S	U	B	W	A	Y	T
R	Y	T	Y	A	Y	P	A	O
A	W	A	Y	Y	M	A	Y	D
Y	A	Y	P	L	A	Y	Y	A
W	E	D	N	E	S	D	A	Y

B1

1 faraway   2 always   3 Bombay   4 haystack   5 Friday   6 decay
7 delay   8 essay   9 daytime   10 playful   11 midday   12 hurray
13 yesterday   14 runaway   15 driveway

C1

1 playful   2 overstay   3 sideways   4 plaything   5 Wednesday
6 haystack   7 repayment   8 yesterday   9 layperson   10 ashtrays

5.3 'ai'

Lesson plan

Note:
The first part of this unit introduced the spelling pattern that is found *most* frequently when the sound /eɪ/ is heard in the middle of a one-syllable word and followed by the sound of a single consonant. In this lesson we look at another common way of spelling the /eɪ/ sound, which is 'ai'. This spelling pattern is generally followed by the letters 'l', 'n' ('nt'), 'r', and sometimes 'm', 'd', 't' and 'se', as in *fail, rain, fair, aim, maid, wait* and *praise*.

1   ELICIT: Ask students to suggest one-syllable words that have the /eɪ/ sound in the middle and are followed by the letter 'l', 'n', or 'r'. Write the words on the board. Possible examples:

   sail   nail   pain   rain   hair   pair

   Now elicit words that end in the sounds 'm', 'd', 't' or 'se'. Possible examples:

   claim   maid   wait   raise

   What spelling pattern can we deduce from this? Note students' suggestions.

2 WRITE ON THE BOARD:

> When we hear 'a' saying its name in the middle of a
> one-syllable word, our second choice is to write
> 'ai'.

Suggest that students copy this and example words into their notebooks.

Note:

There are some homonyms – words that sound the same – that follow both the 'ai' and 'a-e' spelling patterns. Write the following on the board:

maid – made   sail – sale

Ask the students to add some examples of their own, giving the correct meaning of each word in the pair.

Warm-up practice of 'ai' spelling pattern

* *Beginners*

The purpose of this listening exercise is to strengthen the aural-visual awareness of the sound /eɪ/ when it is spelled 'ai' in the middle of the word.

As you read out each of the following pairs of words, students should write down whether they heard the 'ai' word first or second. For an additional challenge, some of your students may want to write the 'ai' words in full.

train – tray   jam – jail   chair – cheek   rain – run   pet – paint
spin – Spain   are – air   brain – bring   fail – full   Fred – afraid

* *Intermediate*

Using the same word pairs, have the students write out all the words in full.

* *Advanced*

In each of the following sentences is a pair of homonyms. Instruct the students to write down both homonyms in the order that they hear them.

1 The **plane** landed on the **plain**.
2 The **pale** man sat on the **pail**.
3 The **maid** in the hotel **made** the bed.

136

4 Sam bought a new **sail** for his boat at the **sale**.
5 You will see the sun's **rays** if you **raise** your head.

A Beginners

1 Sentence search

Write the following words on the board:

**her   is   the   of   rain   Spain   chair   sat   umbrella   maid
in   under   train   waited   on   a**

Ask the students to make as many logical sentences as they can from these words, within five minutes, for example, *The maid sat on a chair*.

At the end of the given time, students read out their sentences.

---

2 Fair game

Write the words represented by the pictures on the right in their correct places in the grid. Do at least eight.

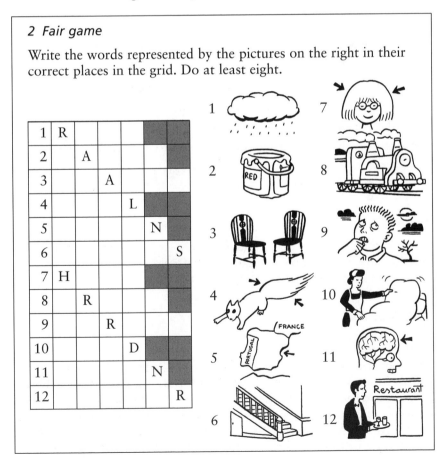

1	R				
2		A			
3			A		
4				L	
5					N
6						S
7	H				
8		R			
9			R		
10				D	
11					N
12						R

© Cambridge University Press 2000

B Intermediate

1 Homonym pairs

Circle one of the homonyms in the brackets to complete the following sentences correctly. Do as many as you can.

1 You are looking very (pail – pale) today. Don't you feel well?
2 Don't cheat! That's just not (fair – fare)!
3 Open the (gait – gate) in order to go into the field.
4 Let me tell you the (plain – plane) truth.
5 I got two letters and a package in my (mail – male) today.
6 Charles Dickens wrote *A (Tail – Tale) of Two Cities*.
7 In order to get to the second floor, walk up those (stairs – stares).
8 Is that a rabbit or a (hair – hare) running across the field?
9 Tell me the (weight – wait) of your suitcase, please.
10 I bought my new jeans in a (sail – sale) at the store.
11 There are many scary rides at the (fair – fare).
12 We (maid – made) some cards for mother's birthday.
13 The (mane – main) idea is to spell correctly!
14 (Rays – Raise) your hand if you want to answer the question.

© Cambridge University Press 2000

2 A to Z

Going through the alphabet, students write an 'ai' word for at least 15 initial letters, for example, A – air; B – bait; etc.

You can compare lists, then report to the class.

C Advanced

1 Storytime

Read out the following story and ask the students to write down as many of the words they can that follow the 'ai' spelling pattern. Then, in groups of three or four, ask the students to combine their words and try to rewrite the story that was narrated to them. Each group must then finish the story and try to add some 'ai' words of their own. The groups take turns in reading out their story to the rest of the class.

Once upon a time there was a wealthy wine-grower named Don Pedro. His grapes were the best in all of **Spain**, his wine was **praised** as a gift from heaven.

One day, Don Pedro called his two sons and spoke to them **plainly**: 'Our family cannot **complain**. We want for nothing. But lately, as I watch you both work hard from sunrise to sunset, I feel ashamed of myself. You both have had no time to look for wives, and set up your own **domains**. Tomorrow night I have arranged for a feast to celebrate the end of the harvest.' The two brothers said not a word, but went **straight** back to their work, happy in the thought that the next evening they would dance and sing and make merry.

Word soon got out that Don Pedro was looking for two brides for his sons. Women from all around **obtained** from Maria, Don Pedro's servant, **details** of what the two sons liked and disliked. That night, under lanterns strung over the yard, dozens of farmers, their families and, of course, their daughters, could not **contain** their excitement. Don Pedro's two sons had seemed interested in everyone they had danced with. The **maid**, Maria, rushed back and forth with wine and food. Then as the night turned into dawn, the guests reluctantly said their goodbyes and left. The two sons **remained** alone in the courtyard with their father.

'Well?' asked Don Pedro.

'We can't **explain** it. Although the local daughters were very beautiful, neither of us could decide.' They hung their heads in shame.

'Then I will help you both choose. It will be in the hands of God. The next woman either of you meet will be your bride.'

At that moment, a **chair** moved. In the shadows stood the **maid**, her thick **braids** slightly glistening in the early morning **rain**. Her beauty glowed, and she was far from **plain**. She walked towards Don Pedro and his two sons, and softly looked into Don Pedro's eyes. 'Which one, sir?'

The sound 'a' (/eɪ/)

Suggested words for spelling test

Some of these words have homonyms, so you could also say the meaning of the problematic words or include them in a meaningful sentence, as they are dictated.

1 *Beginners*
   These words follow the 'ai' spelling pattern only.

rain	paint	hair	wait	Spain
tail	air	train	fair	fail

2 *Intermediate*
   These words all follow the 'ai' spelling pattern, but in addition some have prefixes and suffixes.

again	praising	painful	jailer	contain
fainted	saintly	maiden	failing	nail
retrain	stain	upstairs	plainly	painting

3 *Advanced*
   These words all follow the 'ai' spelling pattern, but some compound words also include previous spelling patterns, prefixes and suffixes.

railway	prepaid	airmail	reclaim	affair
hairspray	detail	faithful	maintain	tailgate
airtight	fairway	waistline	brainwave	explain

Answers

A2

1 rain   2 paint   3 chairs   4 tail   5 Spain   6 stairs   7 hair
8 train   9 afraid   10 maid   11 brain   12 waiter

B1

1 pale   2 fair   3 gate   4 plain   5 mail   6 Tale   7 stairs   8 hare
9 weight   10 sale   11 fair   12 made   13 main   14 raise

6 The sound 'o' (/əʊ/)

6.1 'o-e'

Lesson plan

This unit covers the three most common spelling patterns for the /əʊ/ sound, as in *bone*, *grow* and *boat*. This lesson introduces the spelling pattern that is found most frequently when the sound /əʊ/ is heard in the middle of a one-syllable word and followed by the sound of a single consonant: the Magic – or Silent – 'E' pattern. Note that words spelled with an 'r', like *more*, *score* and *store*, do not, in fact, have the /əʊ/ sound at all, but /ɔː/.

1 ELICIT: Ask students to suggest one-syllable words that have the /əʊ/ sound in the middle and are followed by the sound of a single consonant. Write the words on the board. Possible examples:

bone   hope   globe   home   stone

Common exceptions

The common exceptions for most pronunciations are **folk** and **yolk**.
    If words such as **boat** or **goal** are suggested, write them separately on the board, since they are words that do not follow this spelling pattern but will be introduced later.

2 ASK: What spelling pattern can we deduce from this? Note students' suggestions.

3 WRITE ON THE BOARD:

> When we hear 'o' saying its name in the middle of a one-syllable word followed by a single consonant sound, our first choice is to write
>
> 'o-e'.

Adding a suffix

You might like to remind your students that we drop the final 'e' of a base word before adding a suffix that begins with a vowel, for example,

close + ing = closing   hope + ed = hoped   broke + en = broken

Suggest that students copy this and the exceptions into their notebooks.

Warm-up practice of 'o-e' spelling pattern

* Beginners
The purpose of this listening exercise is to strengthen the visual-aural awareness of the /əʊ/ sound. The table below can be written on the board for the students to copy into their notebooks, and then to fill in the missing consonants as you read out the following words:

smoke   tone   home   rope   close   Rome   nose   bone
stone   globe

1	o	e
2	o	e
3	o	e
4	o	e
5	o	e
6	o	e
7	o	e
8	o	e
9	o	e
10	o	e

* Intermediate
This listening exercise practises the auditory differentiation between the sound /eɪ/ as in *game*, the sound /aɪ/ as in *fine* and the sound /əʊ/ as in *home*.

Draw the following grid on the board for the students to copy into their notebooks.

	a-e	i-e	o-e
1			
2			
3			

As you read the following words, students mark the correct column according to the vowel sound they have heard:

**drive   race   made   broke   line   pope   globe
male   cone   like**

* *Advanced*

Using the same grid and the same words as in the previous exercise, students write the word they hear in the correct column.

A Beginners

1 Lettermix

To find each correct answer, follow the three clues: a picture, a sentence and mixed-up letters. Do at least seven.

1   His home is in Rome.
    He is called the E P P O. __ __ __ __

2   This face has no S N O E. __ __ __ __

3   The Little Prince lived L A N E O.

    __ __ __ __ __ __

4 Go to the O T R S E _ _ _ _ _
to buy some milk.

5 What do dogs like? N S O E B
_ _ _ _ _

6 Jim is talking to Sue on the P O H E N.
_ _ _ _ _ _

7 Where is Joe's bike?
At O H M E. _ _ _ _

8 Mary tells good E S J K O.
_ _ _ _ _

9 If you want to swim, go to the sea-
R E O S H. _ _ _ _ _ _

10 This is Morse E D O C. _ _ _ _

2 Code words

Each letter of the alphabet is represented by a number in the code below.

A	B	C	D	E	F	G	H	I	J	K	L	M
1	2	3	4	5	6	7	8	9	10	11	12	13

N	O	P	Q	R	S	T	U	V	W	X	Y	Z
14	15	16	17	18	19	20	21	22	23	24	25	26

Read the written clues to find the missing words. Some letters you can find by referring back to the code above. Do at least nine.

1 What do you write in?

N	O	T	E	B	O	O	K
14		20	5	2		15	

2 A cold fizzy drink, also called 'cola'.

	3		5

3 Where is the top of the world?

14	15		20				15	12

4 What goes up but never comes down?

19	13		11

5 '

	12	15	20	8	

make the man.'

6 Capital city of Italy.

	13	5

7 He was in the desert for 40 years.

13		19	

8 'My love is like a red, red

18	15		

.'

9 '☐☐☐☐ is where the heart is.'
   (13 | 5)

10 'People who live in
   glass houses shouldn't throw ☐☐☐☐☐☐ ,'
   (19 | | | 14 | 5 | 19)

11 The opposite of 'open' is ☐☐☐☐☐☐ .
   (| 12 | 19 | 4)

12 Instead of words, music uses ☐☐☐☐☐ .
   (14 | 15 | |)

B Intermediate

1 Verbsearch

a. The second form – the Past Simple – of the following verbs all follow the 'o-e' spelling pattern. Find their second form in the grid and write them on the line next to the verbs. Search from left to right and from top to bottom. You can use your dictionaries to look up the meaning of new words and their past form. Do at least 12.

C	H	O	S	E	A	S	W	O	R	E	S
O	K	W	P	X	R	F	R	O	Z	E	T
E	R	T	O	Z	O	Q	O	W	K	T	R
T	W	O	K	E	S	S	T	O	L	E	O
W	O	R	E	K	E	X	E	V	O	P	V
O	S	E	Q	B	R	O	K	E	G	O	E
R	D	R	O	V	E	H	O	R	O	D	E

break	BROKE	strive	....
choose	....	swear	....
drive	....	tear	....
freeze	....	wake	....
ride	....	wear	....
rise	....	weave	....
speak	....	write	....
steal	....		

b. Working with a partner, write a story using at least ten of the past forms of these verbs. The partners take turns writing sentences that continue the story.

---

2 Fan letters

a. How many four-letter and five-letter words can you find from the letters in the fan of cards? You can start either with the letter 'S' in the first card or a letter from the second card of the fan. Use one letter from each section of the fan when forming your words. Try to find at least 12.

'a-e' words	'i-e' words	'o-e' words
....	....	....
....	....	....
....	....	....
....	....	....
....	....	....
....	....	

'a-e' words	*'i-e' words*	*'o-e' words*
....	....	....
....	....	....
....	....	....
....	....	....

b. Some of the words in exercise a are the missing words that fit the following quotes, proverbs and famous rhymes. Write the missing word in the space provided. Find at least five.

1 (*There's*) no fire without some .... (16th century)

2 .... the rod and spoil the child. (Proverbs 13:24)

3 Deeds are .... and words are female. (16th century)

4 As mad as a March .... (14th century)

5 To kill two birds with one .... (17th century)

6 There was a young lady from Riga
Who went for a ride on a tiger,
They returned from the ride,
With the lady inside,

And a .... on the face of the tiger. (Anonymous)

7 Oliver Twist has asked for .... (Charles Dickens)

8 A miss is as good as a .... (19th century)

9 .... away my good name and ....
(*same word*) away my life. (17th century)

10 There was an old owl liv'd in an oak
The more he heard the less he ....
The less he .... , (*same word*) the more he heard
O, if men were all like this wise bird. (*Punch*)

C Advanced

1 Trivia time

a. As an oral exercise, your teacher will give both the definition and the offered choices. You write down or respond orally with the correct 'o-e' word.
OR
b. As individual or pair work, find the word which fits the definition from the offered choices. Use dictionaries to help where possible. Do at least 15.

1 What does *Star Trek*'s Captain Kirk affectionately call the crew doctor? (Bones, Hopeless, Dr Joke)
2 Of which rock group is Mick Jagger the lead singer? (Guns 'n Roses, Smoke, Rolling Stones)
3 To where, according to the old saying, do all roads lead? (Rome, home, the South Pole)
4 'There is no ... without fire.' What word is missing? (coke, smoke, vote)
5 What is the name of the famous Harlem basketball team? (Globetrotters, Nosedivers, Harlem Hopefuls)
6 What might you use to start a car on a cold morning? (yoke, periscope, choke)
7 On a golf course there are 18 ... (strokes, domes, holes)
8 What do the ears and the brain have in common? They both have ... (lobes, globes, moles)
9 What title does the head of the Catholic church have? (pope, Father Rome, Lord of the Throne)
10 What kind of brass musical instrument has a sliding rod? (xylophone, trombone, saxophone)
11 What connects a computer to a telephone line? (prober, modem, spoke)
12 Which fish is found on the underside of your shoes? (That's a joke ...) (sole, smoked salmon, boneless haddock)
13 You can park your car in front of your room at a ... (hotel, motel, yokel)
14 In US slang a man might be called a 'guy'. What is he called in Britain? (smoke, crone, bloke)
15 With what pipe could you clean a car or water the garden? (rose, frozen, hose)
16 What is like a coin and can be used to get on a subway or for a phone? (moke, token, poker)

17 What would we call an animal that has been artificially duplicated? (probe, clone, cyclone)
18 What is a poem that praises something called? (lope, abode, ode)
19 Ecologists are worried about the growing hole in the ... layer. (baritone, ozone, gramophone)
20 What is a task that must be done and might be boring? (chore, folklore, parole)

2 Posers

There are several prefixes that can be added to the word **pose**, changing its meaning:

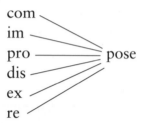

com
im
pro
dis
ex
re

pose

Choose the correct word – **prefix + pose** – to answer each question.

1 Which **pose** means 'to get rid of'? ....

2 Which **pose** means 'to relax'? ....

3 Which **pose** means 'to create music'? ....

4 Which **pose** means 'to show; uncover'? ....

5 Which **pose** means 'to offer'? ....

6 Which **pose** means 'to force; take advantage of'?

....

Now use your dictionary to find the meanings of these other **pose** words:

depose   ....   decompose   ....

suppose   ....   interpose   ....

transpose   ....

Suggested words for spelling test

1 *Beginners*
These words follow the 'o-e' spelling pattern only.

bone	home	stone	joke	rose
pope	smoke	hole	nose	hope

2 *Intermediate*
These words all follow the 'o-e' spelling pattern, but in addition some have prefixes and suffixes.

woke	broken	voter	those	choked
rewrote	hopeful	storing	stole	closed
smoking	chosen	Rome	phone	notebook

3 *Advanced*
These words all follow the 'o-e' spelling pattern, but some compound words also include previous spelling patterns, prefixes and suffixes.

disclose	hopeless	misquote	imposing	enclosed
trombone	ozone	homesick	wholesome	prose
moreover	stoneware	smokestack	roped	monotone

Answers

A1

1 pope   2 nose   3 alone   4 store   5 bones   6 phone   7 home
8 jokes   9 shore   10 code

A2

2 coke   3 North Pole   4 smoke   5 clothes   6 Rome   7 Moses
8 rose   9 Home   10 stones   11 closed   12 notes

B1a

break – broke	choose – chose	drive – drove
freeze – froze	ride – rode	rise – rose
speak – spoke	steal – stole	strive – strove
swear – swore	tear – tore	wake – woke
wear – wore	weave – wove	write – wrote

C	H	O	S	E	A	S	W	O	R	E	S
O	K	W	P	X	R	F	R	O	Z	E	T
E	R	T	O	Z	O	Q	O	W	K	T	R
T	W	O	K	E	S	S	T	O	L	E	O
W	O	R	E	K	E	X	E	V	O	P	V
O	S	E	Q	B	R	O	K	E	G	O	E
R	D	R	O	V	E	H	O	R	O	D	E

B2a

These are the words that we found, but your intermediate students will probably find fewer.

five-letter words

shake   share   spare   stale   stake   stare
shine   shire   smile   spike   spine   spire   spit   stile
shone (note pronunciation!)   shore   smoke   spoke   spore   stoke
stole   stone   store

four-letter words

hare   make   male   mane   mare   pale   pane   pare   tale   take
hike   Mike   mile   mine   pike   pile   pine   tire   tile
hole   mole   more   poke   pole   pore   tone   tore

B2b

1 smoke   2 Spare   3 male   4 hare   5 stone   6 smile   7 more
8 mile   9 Take, take   10 spoke, spoke

C1

1 Bones   2 Rolling Stones   3 Rome   4 smoke   5 Globetrotters
6 choke   7 holes   8 lobes   9 pope   10 trombone   11 modem
12 sole   13 motel   14 bloke   15 hose   16 token   17 clone
18 ode   19 ozone   20 chore

C2

1 dispose   2 repose   3 compose   4 expose   5 propose   6 impose

6.2 '-ow'

Lesson plan

Note:
In this lesson we shall be looking at the most common way of spelling the sound /əʊ/ at the end of a word, which is '-ow'. Your students will know many words where the '-ow' says /aʊ/ as in *cow*, *how*, etc. Remind them that this unit deals with the spelling of the sound /əʊ/, therefore only words with this sound will be presented.

1 ELICIT: Ask students to suggest words that have the sound /əʊ/ at the end. Write the words on the board. Possible examples:

    snow   yellow   tomorrow   grow

Common exceptions

If the following words are suggested, write them in a separate column on the board because they are irregular and should be learnt globally:

    go so also no oh toe hoe roe doe Joe oboe woe hero zero though although dough sew

2 ASK: What spelling pattern can we deduce from this? Note students' suggestions.

3 WRITE ON THE BOARD:

> When we hear 'o' saying its name at the end of
> a word, our first choice is to write
> '-ow'.

Suggest that students copy this and the exceptions into their notebooks.

Warm-up practice of '-ow' spelling pattern

* *Beginners*
The purpose of this listening exercise is to strengthen the visual-auditory awareness of the long vowel sound /əʊ/. The table over can be written on the board for the students to copy into their notebooks.

As you call out the words, the students then check off the appropriate column. Some of your students may feel ready to write out the words in full and should be encouraged to do so.

smoke   snow   yellow   home   window   joke   tomorrow grow   hole   low

	o-e	-ow
1		
2		
3		

* Intermediate
This listening exercise practises the visual-auditory awareness of three long vowel sounds at the end of words: /əʊ/ as in *grow*, /aɪ/ as in *fly* and /eɪ/ as in *day*.

Draw the following grid on the board for the students to copy into their notebooks.

	-ow	-y	-ay
1			
2			
3			

As you read the following words, students mark the correct column according to the vowel sound they have heard. You may want to encourage the more capable students to write the words out in full.

dry   tray   may   show   fly   shadow   throw   stay   deny arrow

* Advanced
Using the same grid as in the previous exercise, students write the word they hear in the correct column. You may want to give the students more difficult words. If so, here are a few suggestions:

'-ow' words:
   widow   bungalow   overthrow   glow   snowman

'-y' words:
   justify   multiply   sly   occupy   qualify

'-ay' words:
   betray   playing   midday   decay   always

A Beginners

1 Picture identification

a. Write the word by its correct picture, for example, *A – follow*. Do at least 12. If you can, first do it without looking at the word list.

1 elbow   2 shadow   3 window   4 snowman   5 blow
6 arrow   7 pillow   8 know   9 below   10 follow
11 throw   12 slow   13 row   14 grow   15 show

b. Use some of the words from the previous exercise to complete these sentences.

1 When I stand in the sun I can see my black ...*shadow*........... .

2 Play baseball and .... the ball.

3 Robin Hood shoots ....s from his bow.

4 Close the .... – it's cold!

5 .... down – the road is dangerous.

6 Do you .... what time it is? It's late!

7 I love winter because I can build a ....

8 My brother and I love to have .... fights when we go to bed.

9 It's very cold. It's twelve degrees .... zero.

10 .... me. I'll show you the way home.

B Intermediate

1 Three in a row

a. Students complete the third word of each category by suggesting a suitable '-ow' word. You might like to do this activity orally, having the students spell out the word, or ask the students to write their answers in their notebooks.

1 Above, beside and *below.*

2 Yesterday, today and ....

3 Stop, give way and ....

4 Door, wall and ....

5 Kick, catch and ....

6 Red, blue and ....

7 Pad, cushion and ....

8 Steal, lend and ....

9 Eat, chew and ....

10 Arm, hand and ....

b. You might like to have the students work in pairs and come up with more categories to share with the class.

2 Follow the idiom

Choose one of the following '-ow' words to complete the idiomatic expressions that match the different definitions. Write the word you choose in the box. Use your dictionary and do at least ten.

window   elbow   grow   shadow

below   row   slow   blow

bow   know   narrow   low

Snow   follow   yellow   show

#			
1		boxing	To fight or box with yourself.
2		motion	Less than normal speed.
3		zero	Minus ten degrees, for example.
4		minded	Someone who won't accept other ideas.
5		shopping	Only looking – not buying.
6		your nose	To do what your heart tells you.

157

The sound 'o' (/əʊ/)

7	up	To become an adult.
8	White	A friend of the Seven Dwarfs.
9	pages	Telephone book for businesses.
10	your boat	Use oars, not a motor, to move your boat.
11	up	To inflate, put air inside.
12	and arrow	Robin Hood's weapon.
13	off	To try to impress.
14	how	Having knowledge.
15	tide	When the sea is far from the coast.
16	room	Having a lot of space.

C *Advanced*

1 *Row, row, row*

All the answers to the following definitions include the word ROW. Answer the definitions and write the letters on the dashes. Try to do seven.

Which ROW word means ...

	... a zucchini-like vegetable	<u>M</u> <u>A</u> <u>R</u> R O W
1	... a missile from a bow	__ __ R O W
2	... an underground hole and tunnel	__ __ __ R O W
3	... great sadness	__ __ __ R O W
4	... to get bigger	__ R O W
5	... to depose, as a political leader	__ __ __ __ __ __ R O W
6	... a three-wheeled wagon that is pushed along	__ __ __ R O W
7	... a black bird	__ R O W
8	... to take, with the intention of returning	__ __ __ R O W
9	... the day after today	__ __ __ __ __ R O W
10	... a small, brown bird	__ __ __ __ R O W

2 *Crossword*

Solve the clues with the help of your dictionary and complete the crossword puzzle.

Across

1 A small, one-storeyed house.
6 Great sadness.
7 Move smoothly.
8 The colour of the sun.
9 Figure to build out of snow.
10 Be aware of.
12 Take for a short time.
14 In a house, made of glass.
15 A 'weeping' tree.
16 In order to pass the ball, you have to ... it.
17 A continuous warm light.

The sound 'o' (/əʊ/)

Down

2 Not wide.
3 Not high.
4 Lie or roll about in water or mud.
5 A large, black bird.

6 Not deep.
11 A woman whose husband has died.
12 A knot in shoelaces.
13 Needing to repay money.

Suggested words for spelling test

1 *Beginners*

These words follow the '-ow' spelling pattern only.

yellow	slow	elbow	show	arrow
grow	window	snow	follow	know

2 *Intermediate*

These words follow the '-ow' spelling pattern, but in addition some have suffixes.

below	slower	followed	pillow	narrower
borrowing	grown	shadowy	snowman	blowing
sparrow	overthrow	rows	sorrowful	tomorrow

3 Advanced

These words follow the '-ow' spelling pattern, but some compound words also include previous spelling patterns, prefixes and suffixes.

showplace	ownership	snowstorm	narrowing	blowtorch
marrow	hollowed	fellowship	scarecrow	mellow
undertow	lawnmower	stowaway	bungalow	knowingly

Answers

A1a

A follow B elbow C shadow D slow E row F snowman
G show H arrow I below J throw K blow L window
M pillow N grow O know

A1b

1 shadow 2 throw 3 arrows 4 window 5 Slow 6 know
7 snowman 8 pillow 9 below 10 Follow

B1a

1 below 2 tomorrow 3 slow 4 window 5 throw 6 yellow
7 pillow 8 borrow 9 swallow 10 elbow

B2

1 shadow 2 slow 3 below 4 narrow 5 window 6 follow
7 grow 8 Snow 9 yellow 10 row 11 blow 12 bow 13 show
14 know 15 low 16 elbow

C1

1 arrow 2 burrow 3 sorrow 4 grow 5 overthrow 6 barrow
7 crow 8 borrow 9 tomorrow 10 sparrow

C2

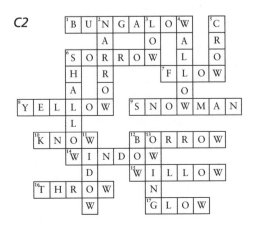

6.3 'oa'

Lesson plan

Note:

In this lesson we shall be looking at the second choice of spelling the sound /əʊ/ in the middle of a word, which is 'oa', as in *boat*. There are about 50 basic words in the English language that follow this spelling pattern. Because there is no rule that governs the choice of spelling the sound /əʊ/ as either 'o-e' or 'oa', you might like to write a short word list on the board, suited to the vocabulary level of the class before going on to the pattern.

1 WRITE ON THE BOARD:

boat   moan   coat   road   goal   coach

2 ASK: What spelling pattern can we deduce from this? Note students' suggestions.

3 WRITE ON THE BOARD:

> When we hear 'o' saying its name in the middle
> of a one-syllable word, our second choice
> is to write
> 'oa'.

Suggest that students copy this into their notebooks.

Warm-up practice of 'oa' spelling pattern

* Beginners

The purpose of this listening exercise is to strengthen the visual-auditory awareness of the sound /əʊ/ when it is written 'oa'.

Read out the following words and ask the students to write them in full in their notebooks. Alternatively, for a less able class, you can write the words on the board and at random call out a word which the students have to copy and write into their notebooks.

goat   road   boat   throat   soap   goal   toast   loaf   coat coach

* *Intermediate*

This listening exercise practises the auditory differentiation between the sound /əʊ/ in the middle of the word, written 'oa' and words that have similar sounding phonemes.

As you read out the following pairs of words, students identify and write down only the 'oa' word.

**load – lot   toss – toast   got – goat   coat – cut   goal – girl
catch – coach   bird – board   bat – boat   soup – soap
read – road**

* *Advanced*

Using the same words as in the previous exercise, students write both words of the pairs.

A Beginners

---

1 Sentence pictures

Tick the sentence which best suits the picture. Do at least seven.
Example:

	a There is a boat on the sea.	
	b The boat is on the rocks.	✓
	c The rocks are on the boat.	

	a Soap is a food.	
	b We wash the dog with soap.	
1	c Don't put soap in the sea: it kills fish.	

	a Play tennis and score a goal.	
	b Play baseball and score a goal.	
2	c Play soccer and score a goal.	

	a 'Where's my coat?' 'It's in the cupboard.'	
	b They have nice, warm coats.	
3	c 'Is it cold?' 'Yes. Close the door.'	

4		a	Goats eat leaves from an oak tree.
		b	Goats can eat an oak tree.
		c	Goats eat coats.

5		a	The giraffe has a long coat.
		b	Giraffes like to eat soap.
		c	The giraffe has a sore throat.

6		a	A coach teaches you to do something better.
		b	A coach has four legs.
		c	This coach is red and yellow.

7		a	Coal is a black rock.
		b	Coal is something you eat.
		c	Coal is a black road.

8		a	The toast is on the road.
		b	My toast is ready.
		c	The toast is burning in the toaster.

9		a	There are cars on the road.
		b	This road leads to Rome.
		c	The toad is on the road.

10		a	In the boat there is a toad.
		b	Toads don't eat candy, they eat flies.
		c	This toad is asleep.

2 Rhyme time

a. Circle the words which rhyme with the first one. Remember: rhyme is sound and not just the way a word looks! Do as many as you can.

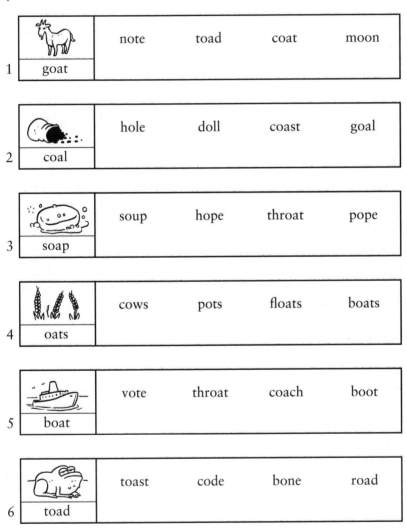

		note	toad	coat	moon
1	goat				

		hole	doll	coast	goal
2	coal				

		soup	hope	throat	pope
3	soap				

		cows	pots	floats	boats
4	oats				

		vote	throat	coach	boot
5	boat				

		toast	code	bone	road
6	toad				

b. Using the words from the previous exercise, write at least five short rhymes, for example, *The boat floats*. Read out and compare your answers with other students.

B Intermediate

Three in one

Brainstorm the class for at least eight words that follow each of the following spelling patterns: 'o-e' in words like *rose*; '-ow' in words like *grow* and 'oa' in words like *road*. Write all the words on the board. You can now do one or more of the following activities with your class:

1 Wordsearch

In their notebooks, students draw a grid of ten squares by eight squares. Using as many of the words as they can, students make up a wordsearch. When ready, they pass their grid on to a friend to solve.

2 Bingo

Using the same grid and instructions from the '-ay' spelling pattern in Unit 5, play 'Bingo'.

3 Erase and spell

Allow the students a few minutes to study the words on the board. Erase the words and let students work in pairs to write as many words as they remember within three minutes. Pairs join together and add to their lists. Report back to class.

C Advanced

1 Story cloze

This is a story cloze, and there is space provided for students to continue the story in their own words. The activity can be done in one of the following three ways:

1 Hand out copies of the cloze and include a word bank for the students to complete on their own.

2 Hand out copies of the cloze without the word bank. Read out the complete story and instruct students to listen carefully without writing anything. Students now have five minutes to complete as many of the missing words as possible, relying on their memory. You might like to have them compare their answers with a partner, before you read the story for a second time.

3 Read out the story in full and ask the students to write down only the words that they think are written with 'oa'. Let the students

compare their word lists with each other. You might want to read out the story more than once. Then let the students rewrite the story in groups, using their word lists. Allow ten minutes for this activity before asking various groups to present their version of the story.

Word bank

> coast   coat   moat   approached
> oatmeal   toast   soaked
> load   groan   throat   coal
> poached   cockroaches   toads

Journey's end

It was 5 am. Captain Daniel was sailing alone along the African
(1) ...., looking for the water channel which would lead
him to the (2) .... mine. As he (3) .... land,
several thousand (4) .... scrambled onto the deck. The
captain's (5) .... tightened and his (6) ....
was soon (7) .... in sweat. He was wet to the bone.
How he hated these insects, even more than his wife hated
(8) ....! A (9) .... escaped his lips. Why had
they sent him here, just for a (10) .... of coal?

   A light flashed out to him from the mainland. Finally he could
enter the port and then follow a channel as narrow as a castle's
(11) .... He sailed up towards the mine. Suddenly he
smiled and licked his lips. Soon he would be able to eat his
favourite breakfast, (12) ...., (13) .... and
(14) .... eggs.

....

....

....

....

....

....

....

....

The end

---

2 Compound choice

Choose the most appropriate word for each definition. Do at least seven. Dictionaries may come in handy.

1. A driver who doesn't allow others to overtake him is called a (cockroach, roadblock, roadhog).
2. It is a type of poisonous fungus. (toadstool, redcoats, cocoa-beans)
3. This person introduces the speaker at a formal dinner. (oarsman, coachman, toastmaster)
4. A place to hang up your coat. (topcoat, cloakroom, coat-tails)
5. Something you can't eat would be (oatmeal, loanshark, potroast).
6. An exciting ride at the funfair is a (roller coaster, coastline, coast guard).
7. You may ride the waves with this. (boathook, oarsman, surfboard)
8. Place to stand on for giving speeches. (soapbox, soapflakes, soapsuds)
9. Where coal is cut out of rock. (coalfield, coalface, coalman)
10. You score between them in football. (goalposts, postmarks, goalkeepers)

Suggested words for spelling test

1 *Beginners*
   These words follow the 'oa' and '-ow' spelling patterns.

yellow	goal	float	coat	slow
boat	road	pillow	throat	coal

2 *Intermediate*
   These words follow the 'oa' and '-ow' spelling patterns, but in addition some have suffixes.

loading	below	coast	coaching	roasted
slowly	foam	floating	narrow	board
goat	following	soapy	toasted	approach

3 *Advanced*
   These words follow all spelling patterns introduced in this unit as well as prefixes, suffixes and compound words.

coalface	elbowing	stolen	reload	toadstool
coastline	moat	approaching	wholesome	sparrows
afloat	cockroach	alone	encroach	abroad

Answers

A1

1c   2c   3b   4a   5c   6a   7a   8c   9b   10b

A2a

1 note – coat   2 hole – goal   3 hope – pope   4 floats – boats
5 vote – throat   6 code – road

C1

1 coast   2 coal   3 approached   4 cockroaches   5 throat
6 coat   7 soaked   8 toads   9 groan   10 load   11 moat
12 oatmeal (toast)   13 toast (oatmeal)   14 poached

C2

1 roadhog   2 toadstool   3 toastmaster   4 cloakroom   5 loanshark
6 roller coaster   7 surfboard   8 soapbox   9 coalface   10 goalposts

7   The sound 'u' (/juː/ and /uː/)

7.1 'u-e'

Lesson plan

This unit will introduce the most common ways of spelling the sounds /juː/ and /uː/. This lesson introduces the spelling pattern that is found most frequently when the sound /juː/ is heard in the middle of a word and followed by the sound of a single consonant.

There are words where the sound /juː/ will be pronounced as /uː/, according to dialect. For example, *duke*, pronounced /djuːk/ in England, may be pronounced /duːk/ in Canada or the USA. There are also words where the preferred pronunciation will be /uː/ for most dialects, for example, *rude, June, flute*. A similar difference in pronunciation may be found in words that follow the other spelling patterns of this unit.

Because there are few 'u-e' words at the beginners' level, we suggest you teach this spelling pattern according to the needs of your students.

1   ELICIT: Ask students to suggest words that have the sound /juː/ or /uː/ and are followed by the sound of a single consonant. The words suggested below are separated according to pronunciation. Write the words on the board.

Possible examples for /juː/:

> **cute   excuse   use   cube   huge**

Possible examples for /uː/:

> **June   rule   rude   Luke**

2   ASK: What spelling pattern can we deduce from this? Note students' suggestions.

3 WRITE ON THE BOARD:

> When we hear 'u' saying its name in a word,
> followed by a single consonant sound,
> our first choice is to write
> 'u-e'.

Adding a suffix

This pattern is another example where you drop the final 'e' before adding a suffix that begins with a vowel, for example,

amuse + 'ing' = amusing   excuse + 'ed' = excused
compute + 'er' = computer

Suggest that students copy this into their notebooks.

Warm-up practice of 'u-e' spelling pattern

* *Intermediate*
This listening exercise practises the auditory differentiation between the following vowel sounds: 'a-e' as in *date*; 'i-e' as in *time*; 'o-e' as in *home* and 'u-e' as in *cute*.
    Draw the following grid on the board for the students to copy into their notebooks.

	a-e	i-e	o-e	u-e
1				
2				
3				

As you read the following words, students mark the correct column according to the vowel sound they have heard.

> rude   quite   plate   tune   stone   lake   amuse   hope   bone
> huge   rule   shine   ace   mule   drive

* *Advanced*
Using the same grid and the same words as in the previous exercise, students write the word they hear in the correct column.

A Intermediate

1 Think of a word

Write the following words on the board:

> **cute volume computer ruler fuse tube June mule excuse cube**

and ask the students to suggest more 'u-e' words to be added to the list. In turn, a volunteer chooses a word without revealing it to the class. S/he gives a definition or association to help the class guess the word which was chosen. After ten students have participated, erase all the words from the board and let the students write down as many words as they remember. Students can then work in pairs to enlarge their lists.

2 Creative headlines

For the class that likes to use its imagination, take the words from the previous exercise and any more that students suggest, to create unusual newspaper headlines, for example, 'Computer Bites Mule'. Students should try to use at least two 'u-e' words in the headlines. Some of the students might like to illustrate the headlines; others can write a story to fit the headline.

B Advanced

1 Word mix

Work out the answers to the definitions with the help of the mixed-up letters. Do at least seven.

Definition	Mixed letters	Answers
1 To say 'no'.	U S E F R E	
2 A musical instrument.	T E L F U	
3 Very big.	G E H U	
4 To make a part of something.	E D C U L N I	

Definition	Mixed letters	Answers
5 To make smaller or lighter.	D R E E C U	☐☐☐☐☐☐
6 British nobleman.	K U D E	☐☐☐☐
7 Measuring stick.	L R U E R	☐☐☐☐☐
8 To make the sick well.	E R C U	☐☐☐☐
9 Mixed-up.	N O F S C D E U	☐☐☐☐☐☐☐☐
10 To end.	L C U N O E D C	☐☐☐☐☐☐☐☐☐

2 The 'use' of words

a. All the answers to the definitions below are words that end in '-use'. Use your dictionary to help you match the right word to each definition. Write the letter of the definition and the whole word on the line. Do at least ten.

  a To join together; a safety device in electricity.
  b To say someone has done something wrong.
  c Someone who has difficulty understanding.
  d To mix up two or more things.
  e To treat badly; to be cruel.
  f To think about for a while; an imaginative, creative force.
  g To pass the time pleasantly.
  h To use incorrectly or dishonestly.
  i To choose not to do something.
  j To give a reason for your behaviour.
  k A deceiving plan.
  l To fill with (hope, for example).
  m To scan.
  n Garbage, rubbish.
  o To puzzle or daze.

1 R		1 RUSE —k
2 BEM		2 ....
3 INF		3 ....
4 AB		4 ....
5 M		5 ....
6 ACC		6 ....
7 AM	+USE	7 ....
8 CONF		8 ....
9 EXC		9 ....
10 F		10 ....
11 REF (noun)		11 ....
12 REF (verb)		12 ....
13 MIS		13 ....
14 OBT		14 ....
15 PER		15 ....

b. Rewrite the following sentences using words from the previous exercise to replace the underlined words or phrases. Sometimes it is necessary to change the form of the word. Do at least seven.

1 The joke was really <u>funny</u> – I had to laugh.

   ....

2 I was rather <u>puzzled</u> by your strange invitation.

   ....

3 Joe <u>said he wouldn't</u> go with me.

   ....

4 <u>Pardon</u> me, madam, may I get past you?

   ....

5 As I was <u>looking through</u> the newspaper I found some interesting articles.

   ....

6 Don't <u>treat</u> your dog <u>badly</u> – it might bite you.

....

7 Sometimes you can be so <u>dull and stupid</u>.

....

8 We must recycle our <u>garbage</u>.

....

9 The old lady was terribly <u>mixed up</u> and lost her way.

....

10 The soldiers were <u>filled</u> with joy when they heard the war was over.

....

© Cambridge University Press 2000

Suggested words for spelling test

1 *Intermediate*

These words all follow the 'u-e' spelling pattern, but in addition some have prefixes and suffixes.

excuse	useful	refusing	tune	Luke
fuse	cube	computer	confused	June
huge	duke	amused	fortune	reduce

2 *Advanced*

useless	immature	produce	contribute	execute
confusing	infused	misuse	altitude	volume
composure	disputed	abusing	computed	endurable

Answers

B1

1 refuse   2 flute   3 huge   4 include   5 reduce   6 duke   7 ruler
8 cure   9 confused   10 conclude

B2a

1 k – ruse   2 o – bemuse   3 l – infuse   4 e – abuse   5 f – muse
6 b – accuse   7 g – amuse   8 d – confuse   9 j – excuse   10 a – fuse
11 n – refuse (n)   12 i – refuse (vb)   13 h – misuse   14 c – obtuse
15 m – peruse

B2b

1 amusing   2 bemused   3 refused to   4 Excuse   5 perusing
6 abuse   7 obtuse   8 refuse   9 confused   10 infused

7.2 '-ue'

Lesson plan

Note:
In this lesson we shall be looking at the most common way of spelling the sounds /juː/ and /uː/ at the end of a word, which is '-ue', as in *rescue* and *true*.

Because there are few '-ue' words at the beginners' level, we suggest you teach this spelling pattern according to the needs of your students.

1 ELICIT: Ask students to suggest words that have the sound /juː/ or /uː/ at the end. Write the words on the board. Possible examples:

blue   glue   rescue   true

Common exceptions

If the following words are suggested, write them in a separate column. They do not follow the spelling pattern and should be taught as global words:

shoe   do   you   to   two   through   canoe   ewe

If words that follow the '-ew' or '-oo' spelling patterns, such as *new* and *too* are suggested, write them in a separate column on the board and explain that they will be introduced later in this unit.

2 ASK: What spelling pattern can we deduce from this? Note students' suggestions.

3 WRITE ON THE BOARD:

> When we hear 'u' saying its name at the end of
> a word, our first choice is to write
> '-ue'.

Adding a suffix

Remind the students that, just as they have learnt in previous units, here, too, the final 'e' is dropped before adding suffixes that begin with a vowel, for example,

rescue + 'ing' = rescuing continue + 'ed' = continued
blue + 'er' = bluer

You might suggest that students add this, together with the spelling pattern and the irregular words, to their spelling notebooks.

Warm-up practice of '-ue' spelling pattern

* Intermediate
The purpose of this listening exercise is to strengthen the visual-auditory perception of the sound /juː/ and /uː/, both in the middle of a word and at the end of a word. The table below can be written on the board for the students to copy into their notebooks. As you call out the words, the students then check off the appropriate column. Some of your students may feel ready to write out the words in full and should be encouraged to do so.

**fuse blue avenue rude cute continue value pure
mule clue**

	u-e	-ue
1		
2		
3		

* Advanced
This listening exercise practises the auditory differentiation between the following spelling patterns: '-ay' as in *day*; '-y' as in *fly*; '-ow' as in *blow* and '-ue' as in *true*.

Draw the following grid on the board for the students to copy into their notebooks.

	-ay	-y	-ow	-ue
1				
2				
3				

The sound 'u' (/juː/ and /uː/)

As you read the following words, students mark the correct column according to the vowel sound they have heard. You may want to encourage the more capable students to write the words out in full.

glue   ally   arrow   continue   yesterday   shy   cue   anyway pursue   crow

A Intermediate

1 Scatterbrain story

a. 'Scatter' the following words on the board:

> blue   rescue   overdue   true
>
> glue   argue   continue   pursue
>
>   clue
>
>   barbecue   statue
>   avenue

Ask the class to suggest more words that follow the '-ue' spelling pattern. Allow the students to look at the words for a few minutes, then erase them from the board. Individually, students should now write down as many words as they remember before pairing up to compare their lists. Have each pair of students join up with a neighbouring pair to complete and check their final lists. (You may like to rewrite all the '-ue' words on the board so that the students can check their accuracy.)

b. Write on the board two or three topics which can be developed into stories, for example, Police Report, The Picnic, etc. The students, still in their groups of four, must 'get rid of' the words on their lists by contributing one or more sentences to develop into an oral story. Make sure that the students take turns until all the words have been used. You might now like to have the students work individually and write down the story developed in their group. Volunteers can read out their stories to the class.

B Advanced

1 Mystery murder

Using some of the words from the word bank, complete the following police dialogue. If you can, finish the story in your own words, implementing '-ue' words wherever possible. You might find a dictionary helpful.

residue	barbecue	true	clue
cue	continue	revenue	value	tissue
glue	Sue	due	statue	Avenue

MYSTERY MURDER

On the night of June 15th, police hurried to an address in East London in answer to a neighbour's phone call. After breaking through the entrance door, they searched the house and found two bodies in the back room. Beside the bodies was a jar of (1) ....

'That's our first (2) ....,' said Sgt Putright. 'Forensic science will have to take a (3) .... sample and send it to the lab.

'OK,' said (4) ...., the criminal investigation officer. 'Get a sample and send it down to the lab on Grasmere (5) ....'

Suddenly, Sgt Putright sniffed the air. 'I smell smoke ... Well, look at that – the neighbours are having a (6) .... in their back yard.'

'Keep your mind on your work, Sergeant, I know you're hungry. But did you notice this wooden (7) .... of Cupid over here? It's probably of great (8) ....' 'That's (9) ....,' agreed Putright. 'I think we'll have to (10) .... our investigation in the neighbours' back yard. We should check the (11) .... in the ashes.'

'You're right.'

At that moment, a scream was heard from the neighbours' back porch ... To be continued BY YOU

2 Triviality

The answers to these clues are all words that follow either the 'u-e' or '-ue' spelling pattern. The lines indicate the number of letters for each answer. Do at least ten.

1 Stick used in billiards or snooker – _ _ _

2 A pill, or part of a spaceship – _ _ _ _ _ _ _

3 Light theatre entertainment, with jokes and dances –

_ _ _ _ _

4 Old-fashioned word for Christmas – _ _ _ _ _

5 Figure made by a sculptor – _ _ _ _ _ _ _

6 Fancy dress; clothes worn by actors – _ _ _ _ _ _ _ _

7 To blame somebody for a crime – _ _ _ _ _ _ _

8 Thin paper; group of body cells – _ _ _ _ _ _ _

9 Street or long, tree-lined road – _ _ _ _ _ _ _

10 A colour – _ _ _ _ _

11 Height, as of a mountain – _ _ _ _ _ _ _ _ _

12 To say 'No' – _ _ _ _ _ _ _

13 To save – _ _ _ _ _ _ _

14 To cook outside over an open fire –

_ _ _ _ _ _ _ _

15 To quarrel – _ _ _ _ _ _

Suggested words for spelling tests

1 *Intermediate*

tissue	rescued	statue	blue	clueless
avenue	continue	argue	glue	value
barbecue	cue	overdue	true	sue

2 *Advanced*
This list includes words that follow both the '-ue' and 'u-e' spelling pattern.

continuing	infuse	immature	valuable	residue
altitude	duke	argument	tissue	volume
subdued	refusal	bluer	venue	issue

Answers

B1

1 glue   2 clue   3 tissue   4 Sue   5 Avenue   6 barbecue   7 statue
8 value   9 true   10 continue   11 residue

B2

1 cue   2 capsule   3 revue   4 Yule   5 statue   6 costume   7 accuse
8 tissue   9 avenue   10 blue   11 altitude   12 refuse   13 rescue
14 barbecue   15 argue

7.3 '-ew'

Lesson plan

Note:
In this lesson we shall be looking at the second choice for spelling the sounds /juː/ and /uː/ at the end of a word, which is '-ew', as in *view* and *drew*.

Because there are few '-ew' words at the beginners' level, we suggest you teach this spelling pattern according to the needs of your students.

1 REMIND students of the previous lesson where they learnt the most common way of spelling the sounds /juː/ and /uː/ at the end of a word: '-ue'. Ask students to recall some of these words. Write the words on the board. Possible examples:

   blue   glue   rescue   true

2 EXPLAIN that in this lesson they are going to be introduced to the second choice for spelling these sounds at the end of a word: '-ew'.

3 ASK students if they know of any words that end in '-ew', and write their suggestions on the board, for example,

   new   grew   few   nephew

4 WRITE ON THE BOARD:

> When we hear 'u' saying its name at the end of
> a word, our second choice is to write
> '-ew'.

You might suggest that students add this spelling pattern to their notebooks.

Warm-up practice of '-ew' spelling pattern

* *Intermediate and advanced*
This listening exercise practises the auditory differentiation between the following spelling patterns: '-ay' as in *day*; '-y' as in *fly*; '-ow' as in *blow* and '-ew' as in *few*.

Write on the board the following groups of letters and ask the students to copy them into their notebooks:

dr___ dr___　　cr___ cr___　　m___ m___　　sl___ sl___
gr___ gr___　　fl___ fl___　　st___ st___　　kn___ kn___

Now write on the board the following 'endings', reviewing each sound:

-ay -y -ow -ew

Read out the following words in their pairs and ask the students to add the appropriate endings in their notebooks, according to what they hear:

drew – dry　　crow – cry　　my – may　　slay – slew
grow – grew　　fly – flow　　stew – stow　　knew – know

A Intermediate

1 Up, down, left, right

The answers to the clues are all in the grid and follow either the 'u-e', '-ue' or '-ew' spelling patterns. You must start at the letter given (in the grid it will have a dot in the corner of its square) and then move one square in any direction – up, down, left or right – changing direction when necessary, in order to discover the words. Do at least ten.

© Cambridge University Press 2000

T	W	E	R	N	A	C	R	P	D
U	N	I	E	B	V	S	E	K	U
R	E	V	U	N	E	M	W	S	A
P	R	E	N	T	L	U	C	S	H
S	U	C	O	I	L	G	W	I	N
E	E	X	U	N	U	R	E	J	F
U	L	B	M	H	E	B	G	W	E

1 Start at T. A melody. _ _ _ _

2 Start at P. Seeing a film before the public does.

_ _ _ _ _ _ _

3 Start at C. To carry on. _ _ _ _ _ _ _ _ _

4 Start at E. To pardon. _ _ _ _ _ _ _

5 Start at H. An ancient language. _ _ _ _ _ _ _

6 Start at R. Income, money. _ _ _ _ _ _ _

7 Start at D. A member of the royal family. _ _ _ _

8 Start at G. Sticky stuff. _ _ _ _

9 Start at S. Like a nail, but twisted into position.

_ _ _ _ _

10 Start at A. A tree-lined street. _ _ _ _ _ _

11 Start at F. Not many. _ _ _

12 Start at B. A colour. _ _ _ _

13 Start at M. An animal related to the horse. _ _ _ _

2 Searching for verbs

Complete the sentences with a suitable verb, then find the verbs in the wordsearch. They are all past tenses: some are regular and end with an '-ed', others irregular and end with '-ew'. Search from left to right and from top to bottom. Try to find nine.

1 Sam was a thin child, but he .... up to be a heavy adult.

2 The pupils .... gum in class yesterday, which was against school rules.

3 The wind was very strong last night and .... down several trees.

4 That girl .... a lovely picture in her art class last week.

5 Our cat .... a lot last night and the noise kept me awake.

6 I .... that woman when she was only a girl.

7 The girls in the basketball team .... the ball into the net ten times, but scored only nine.

8 He wanted to become president, but .... from the elections when it became clear he wouldn't win.

9 That pilot .... around the world in less than 48 hours.

10 We recently .... our subscription to the newspaper: it is well worth reading.

11 Jake .... apples and pears to make a delicious dessert.

12 The Black Knight .... the evil dragon after a brave battle.

W	S	C	H	E	W	E	D	M
F	L	E	W	S	E	D	W	E
W	E	Q	E	T	H	R	E	W
G	W	D	R	E	W	R	K	E
R	E	N	E	W	E	D	N	D
E	W	B	L	E	W	W	E	W
W	I	T	H	D	R	E	W	E

B Advanced

1 Figure the clues

Solve the clues and write your answers, with the clue number, in the correct box, according to the spelling pattern. You may either work with the word bank or, for an extra challenge, try to complete the exercise without peeking! Do at least 15. You might find it helpful to use your dictionary.

1 Removes the cork from a wine bottle.

2 Grown-up and fully developed.

3 A dried plum.

4 Correct, not imagined.

5 Meat, vegetables cooked in a pot.

6 Stone or bronze figure.

7 Fancy dress.

8 To eat or drink something.

9 Part of the electrical system.

10 Written opinion of a new book.

11 To bite many times in your mouth.

12 A paper handkerchief.

13 Your brother's son.

14 To save.

15 Law – be home by 9 pm!

16 Moisture on grass in the morning.

17 Worth of something.

18 A signal to an actor.

19 To say no.

20 To carry on doing something.

21 Reason for not doing something.

u-e	-ew	-ue
....	....	....
....	....	....
....	....	....
....	....	....
....	....	....
....	....	....
....	....	....

dew   volume   fuse   costume

stew   corkscrew   tissue

prune   cue   barbecue   rescue   excuse   consume

mature   curfew   true   crew

statue   continue   chew

review   refuse   nephew   value

2 Alphabet words

Divide the class into three groups. Each group will be assigned one of the spelling patterns covered in this unit: 'u-e', '-ue' and '-ew'. Using dictionaries, each group will be responsible for using the alphabet sequence to start words with their particular spelling pattern. Examples: A – amuse; A – argue; A – askew. (Some letters will be 'orphans', that is, there will be no word which begins with those letters.)

The group with the longest list within ten minutes wins.

Suggested words for spelling tests

1 *Intermediate*

blew	few	news	grew	crew
cashews	threw	knew	view	flew
renew	drew	screw	review	Jew

2 *Advanced*

Students have to differentiate between homonyms, and write the words in the order they hear them in the sentences.
1 I *threw* the ball *through* the window.
2 I *knew* your bike was *new*.
3 *Do* they like the wet *dew* in the morning?
4 She has to *choose* the gum she *chews*.
5 He *blew* the *blue* horn.

Answers

A1

1 tune 2 preview 3 continue 4 excuse 5 Hebrew 6 revenue
7 duke 8 glue 9 screw 10 avenue 11 few 12 blue 13 mule

T	W	E	R	N	A	C	R	P	D
U	N	I	E	B	V	S	E	K	U
R	E	V	U	N	E	M	W	S	A
P	R	E	N	T	L	U	C	S	H
S	U	C	O	I	L	G	W	I	N
E	E	X	U	N	U	R	E	J	F
U	L	B	M	H	E	B	G	W	E

A2

1 grew   2 chewed   3 blew   4 drew   5 mewed   6 knew   7 threw
8 withdrew   9 flew   10 renewed   11 stewed   12 slew

W	S	C	H	E	W	E	D	M
F	L	E	W	S	E	D	W	E
W	E	Q	E	T	H	R	E	W
G	W	D	R	E	W	R	K	E
R	E	N	E	W	E	D	N	D
E	W	B	L	E	W	W	E	W
W	I	T	H	D	R	E	W	E

B1

u-e	-ew	-ue
2 mature	1 corkscrew	4 true
3 prune	5 stew	6 statue
7 costume	10 review	12 tissue
8 consume	11 chew	14 rescue
9 fuse	13 nephew	17 value
19 refuse	15 curfew	18 cue
21 excuse	16 dew	20 continue

7.4 'oo'

Lesson plan

Note:

1 This vowel digraph (two letters which read as one sound) is generally pronounced /uː/ as in *moon*, but there are several common words where 'oo' has the sound /ʊ/ as in *foot*. Most intermediate and advanced students will have little or no problem with this spelling pattern's two different sounds, so the vocabulary in the listening and graded exercises includes both.

2 The most common position for 'oo' is in the middle of a word. It occasionally appears at the beginning or end of words, such as in *ooze* and *zoo*.

3 At the beginner level, the warm-up listening exercise includes words from both sounds since they are common words. This is followed by two written exercises that deal with each sound separately in order to reinforce the vocabulary for both sound patterns. The vocabulary in the third exercise includes both sounds.

1 WRITE ON THE BOARD:

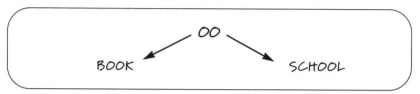

Have the students read the two words silently.

2 ASK: What sounds do we hear with this spelling pattern?

3 ELICIT: Ask students to suggest other 'oo' words for each sound, and write their suggestions on the board in two columns.

Common exceptions

If the following words are suggested, you may want to write them in a separate column since they are irregular:

/uː/ – **group   soup   lose   whose   move   truth   juice   womb
tomb**

/ʊ/ – **could   would   should   put   wolf   pull   bull   full   push**

The following 'oo' words have an irregular pronunciation: **blood, flood, door, floor** and **poor** (in some dialects).

4 ASK: What spelling pattern can we deduce from this? Note students' suggestions. (Since this spelling rule becomes a second choice for the sound /uː/ in the middle of a word and the third choice for the end of a word, you may want to review the spelling patterns in this unit.)

5 WRITE ON THE BOARD:

> When we hear 'u' saying its name in the middle of
> a word, our second choice will be to write
>
> 'oo'.
>
> Sometimes 'oo' can sound like /ʊ/ as in book.

The sound 'u' (/juː/ and /uː/)

Suggest that the students copy this and the exceptions into their notebooks.

Warm-up practice of 'oo' spelling pattern

* *Beginners*
The purpose of this listening exercise is to strengthen the aural-visual awareness of the two sounds of 'oo': /uː/ as in *moon*, and /ʊ/ as in *book*. Write the following words on the board:

> **boot   foot   room   good-bye   cook   school   choose
> wood   balloon   zoo**

Read out words at random. Each student silently tries to identify the correct word and writes it in his/her notebook. For students that are more able, you might suggest they keep their eyes down, and try to write the word without looking at it on the board.

* *Intermediate*
The purpose of this listening exercise is to strengthen the aural-visual awareness of 'oo' when it is pronounced both as *book* and as *moon*.
  Write on the board only first-letter clues to the following words:

> **notebook   cartoons   took   foolish   shoot   childhood   loose
> sooner   toothpaste   stood   baboon   wool   moonlight   poor
> football**

As you call out each word, students write the complete word.

* *Advanced*
The purpose of this listening exercise is to strengthen the aural-visual awareness of 'oo' when it is pronounced both as *book* and as *moon*. On the board, draw the following chart and ask students to copy it into their notebooks.

/uː/ *moon*	/ʊ/ *book*

Read out the following words and ask students to write them in the grid, under the most suitable heading:

> **noose   shook   monsoon   wooden   outlook   misunderstood
> troops   hooves   gloomily   wool   scooter   honeymoon
> crooked   unloosen**

190

A Beginners

---

1 Short word, long word

a. Find compound words or phrases for each of the three 'oo' words (pronounced /ʊ/ as in *wood*) at the top of the grid by using one of the words in the box below. Do as many as you can.

book	foot	good
book club		

> morning   shelf   club   shop   bye   friend
>
> night   steps   store   ball

© Cambridge University Press 2000

b. Elicit other 'oo' words pronounced /ʊ/ as in *good* and have students suggest compound words, idioms or expressions. Additional 'oo' words could include: **wood, cook, look, hood.**

2 Where is the goose?

In each sentence use the picture to identify the missing 'oo' word which must have the sound /uː/, as in *soon*. Write the word in the space provided. When finished, unscramble all of the circled letters to find out: 'Where is the goose?'

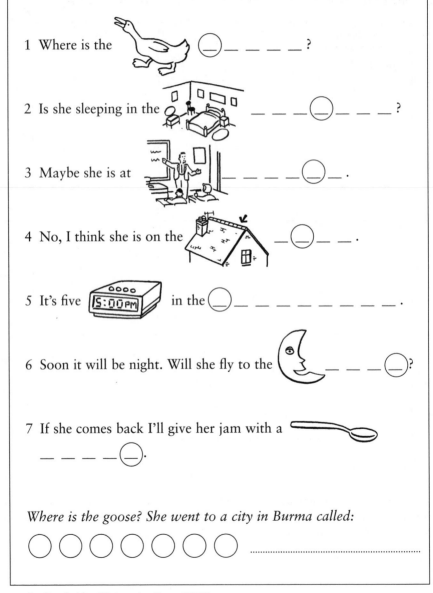

1 Where is the ⬡ _ — — — ?

2 Is she sleeping in the _ — — ⬡ — — — ?

3 Maybe she is at _ — — — ⬡ — .

4 No, I think she is on the _ ⬡ — — .

5 It's five **|5:00 PM|** in the ⬡ — — — — — — — — .

6 Soon it will be night. Will she fly to the — — — ⬡ ?

7 If she comes back I'll give her jam with a

— — — — ⬡ .

Where is the goose? She went to a city in Burma called:

◯ ◯ ◯ ◯ ◯ ◯ ....

3 At the zoo

This exercise can be done in either of two ways. Choose the method which suits the level of your class.

a. Individual or pair work: Read through the story and fill in the missing 'oo' words from the box. Do as many as you can. When you have finished, complete the story in your own words, including at least one more 'oo' word.

OR

b. Your teacher first reads out the story, including the 'answer' words. After listening to the story twice, you then try to fill in the words from memory. You will be given a time limit. Afterwards, work in pairs to compare and complete more answers. Your teacher now reads the story again to allow you to self-check your work.

floor   cartoon   too

footsteps   football

door   kangaroos

afternoon   school

zoo

bedroom

look   poodle

Goodbye   baboons   food

It is three o'clock in the (1) .... I am sitting in my

(2) .... , watching my favourite (3) .... on

the TV. Suddenly, I hear some (4) .... outside. It's Jack,

my friend from (5) .... With him is his dog, Pocka.

Pocka is a (6) ....

    I invite them in and we all sit on the (7) ....

    'Pocka and I want to see the animals in the (8) ....

Do you want to come, (9) ....?' asks Jack.

    'I don't know,' I answer. 'I want to play (10) ....'

'Please come. We can (11) .... at the monkeys, and the (12) .... and the (13) .... Maybe we can give them some (14) .... to eat. It will be fun!'

'OK. Let's go to the zoo. Wait a minute. I have to tell my mum.'

I call out '(15) ...., Mum!!' Then, Jack, Pocka and I go out the front (16) .... In ten minutes we are there. You can't believe what happens next ...

B Intermediate

1 Scoop!

Find the correct compound word for each definition by combining two words, one from each of the boxes below. Start each compound word with a word from the box on the left. Each compound word must contain at least one 'oo' word. Do as many as you can.

child book tooth moon goose bride foot note foot dining school mush cook after tea good	book master bye worm hood spoon rooms groom noon paste room print bumps light book ball

1 A popular team game. ....

2 The time when a person is young. ....

© Cambridge University Press 2000

194

3 The place at home, where you might eat. ....

4 What you might say when you leave. ....

5 You might use it to put sugar in a drink. ....

6 The mark on the ground made by a shoe. ....

7 The time of day between morning and evening.

....

8 You might use this to clean your teeth. ....

9 They grow wild in the forest and are good to eat.

....

10 What you might get on your skin when you are cold or

scared. ....

11 The man who teaches you. ....

12 At night we can see by the ....

13 Where you might write your homework. ....

14 The most important man at a wedding. ....

15 Where you can find lots of recipes. ....

16 A person who reads all the time! ....

2 Circles in the squares

Solve the clues and write the letters of the words in the boxes. The 'oo' in each word will help you. Do as many as you can.

Clue						
1 A place to see animals.					o	o
2 The past of 'take'.				o	o	
3 Not tight.			o	o		
4 A dog with curly fur.		o	o			
5 To select.			o	o		
6 A place of learning.				o	o	
7 An Australian animal.					o	o
8 Sweep the floor with this.				o	o	
9 Knives, forks and ...			o	o		
10 A two-wheeled vehicle.		o	o			
11 Animals in the ape family.			o	o		
12 On top of the house.				o	o	
13 Also; as well as.					o	o

C Advanced

1 One in the middle

a. Write an 'oo' word between each pair of words in order to form a compound word or phrase that ends the first word and starts the second, for example, after .... time.

By adding the word *noon*, you can form the two new words *afternoon* and *noontime*. You can use your dictionary to help you. Do as many as you can.

1 foot .... change

2 April .... proof

3 bath .... mate

4 phone .... shelf

5 good .... glass

6 junk .... processor

7 milk .... paste

8 blue .... light

9 child .... wink

10 pussy .... step

11 night .... bag

12 swimming .... table

b. Now use some of the words you formed to answer these questions:

1 Where could you study in the evenings? ....

2 What is another term for cash or small coins? ....

3 Where could you have a shower? ....

4 What are chips, chocolate and hotdogs sometimes called?

....

5 What is another name for a mirror? ....

6 Where might you practise your backstroke? ....

7 What word means to trick or deceive someone?

....

8 Where might you look up someone's address?

....

2 Look and choose

Write the following grid on the board:

T	C	L
H	oo	M
N	S	P

Instruct students to find as many 'oo' words as possible from the letters in the grid. They should use their dictionary to help them find words that contain at least three letters.

Suggested words for spelling test

The lists include both the /uː/ and /ʊ/ sounds.

1 *Beginners*

book	moon	good	food	wood
cook	tooth	zoo	cool	roof

2 *Intermediate*

understood	proof	scooter	childhood	shook
scoop	foolish	sooner	moonlight	loose
tattoo	bookshelf	good-looking	baboon	poodle

3 *Advanced*
This list includes common exceptions.

manhood	moody	uproot	hoof	outlook
broomstick	gloomily	wooden	wouldn't	monsoon
loosen	juice	brook	loser	footstool

Answers

A1a

bookshop   bookshelf   bookstore   book club
football   footsteps
goodbye   goodnight   good friend   good morning

A2

1 goose   2 bedroom   3 school   4 roof   5 afternoon
6 moon   7 spoon

Where is the goose? She went to a city in Burma called … Rangoon.

A3

1 afternoon   2 bedroom   3 cartoon   4 footsteps   5 school
6 poodle   7 floor   8 zoo   9 too   10 football   11 look
12 kangaroos/baboons   13 baboons/kangaroos   14 food
15 Goodbye   16 door

B1

1 football   2 childhood   3 dining-room   4 goodbye   5 teaspoon
6 footprint   7 afternoon   8 toothpaste   9 mushrooms
10 goosebumps   11 schoolmaster   12 moonlight   13 notebook
14 bridegroom   15 cookbook   16 bookworm

B2

1 zoo   2 took   3 loose   4 poodle   5 choose   6 school
7 kangaroo   8 broom   9 spoons   10 scooter   11 baboons
12 roof   13 too

C1a

1 loose   2 fool   3 room   4 book   5 looking   6 food   7 tooth
8 moon   9 hood   10 foot   11 school   12 pool

C1b

1 night school   2 loose change   3 bathroom   4 junk food
5 looking glass   6 swimming pool   7 hoodwink   8 phone book

C2

We found the following words – there are probably more!

soon   spoon/s   spool/s   sloop/s   shoo   shoot/s   school/s   scoop/s
snoot   stool/s   stoop/s   too   tool/s   toot/s   tooth   cool/s
coop/s   coot/s   moon/s   moot   noon   pool/s   pooch   hoop/s
hoot/s   loop/s   loot   loom/s

8   The sound 'e' (/iː/)

8.1 'ee'

Lesson plan

This unit covers the most common spelling patterns for the sound /iː/, as in *green, meat, funny, chief* and *receive*. In this lesson we look at the spelling pattern 'ee', which is a vowel digraph. (A digraph is two letters which read as one sound.)

Note:

Unfortunately, two of the patterns for the /iː/ sound ('ee', 'ea') are equally common and there is no rule to help us know which one to use.

1   EXPLAIN that there is no rule that tells us whether the sound /iː/ is spelled 'ee' or 'ea' when it is followed by a consonant sound, but in this lesson we will be concentrating on the 'ee' pattern.

2   INTRODUCTION: Write the following words on the board:

>   **green   teeth   jeep   cheese   week**

Ask students to suggest other one-syllable words that have the /iː/ sound in the middle and are followed by the sound of a single consonant.

Common exceptions

If the following words are suggested, write them in a separate column on the board because they are irregular and should be learnt globally:

>   **these   here   scene   scheme**

If words such as **please, clean, chief, piece** or **seize** are suggested, write them separately on the board, since they are words that do not follow this spelling pattern but will be introduced later.

3   ASK: What spelling pattern can we deduce from this? Note students' suggestions.

4 WRITE ON THE BOARD:

> When we hear 'e' saying its name in the middle
> of a one-syllable word, followed by a single consonant
> sound, we often write
> 'ee'.

You might like to write the following words which end in 'ee' on the board. They are common words, but few in number:

tree   see   three   bee   free   knee

Suggest that students copy the spelling pattern and the exceptions into their notebooks.

Warm-up practice of 'ee' spelling pattern

* Beginners
The purpose of this listening exercise is to strengthen the visual-auditory awareness of the /iː/ sound, as in *cheek*. Since speakers of many other languages have trouble distinguishing between the /ɪ/ and /iː/ sounds in English, these drills have particular importance.

In their notebooks, students write the numbers 1–15 in a column. As you read out the following words, instruct the students to write a tick when the word they hear has the sound /iː/, as in *cheek*.

**green   win   need   wheel   well   week   sleep   teeth   chess
fill   feel   ship   sheep   red   queen**

As you review the answers, you may want to have students come and write the words on the board.

* Intermediate
Using the same words as in the previous exercise, students should try to write *all* the words. Explain that the list includes not only the 'ee' pattern, but also words that have a short vowel sound.

* Advanced
Read out the following word pairs and ask the students to write them down as they hear them. Words follow the 'ee' spelling pattern and the short vowel sounds when they are written 'i' or 'e'.

**deep – dip   chess – cheese   sped – speed   seek – sick   fed – feed
feel – fill   fit – feet   deed – did   slip – sleep   teen – ten**

A Beginners

1 'ee' match

a. Use the word bank to write in a suitable 'ee' word for each definition. Some words are 'extra'. Do as many as you can.

teeth	tree	wheels		cheeks
	sweet		sleep	
queen	see			
			street	feet
	week			
		sheep		
keep	three		jeep	green

1 The king's wife. ....

2 In your mouth. ....

3 When you're tired, go to ... .

4 You walk on them. ....

5 A colour. ....

6 To look. ....

7 Seven days. ....

8 A number. ....

9 An animal. ....

10 There are two on your face. ....

11 There are four on a car. ....

12 Apples grow on this. ....

b. Now write a suitable clue for each of the remaining words and let your partner find the answers.

B Intermediate

1 The old woman and the Greek

Write the following words on the board:

feet cheek Greek green jeep meet sleep street freezing
feel sweet weeks geese deep deeper queen teeth

Check to see that all students understand their meanings. Tell the students that they are now going to hear a story that includes all the words that appear on the board. Ask the students to listen carefully because they must remember in what connection the words were used. You can then read out the story several times, preferably in a dramatic manner.

If you ever **meet** a **Greek** named Stephanus, he will probably tell you this story:

"One day I was driving my **jeep** down the **street** when suddenly an ugly, old woman stopped me. She spoke to me in a strange, **deep** voice: 'Please, please help me. For many **weeks** now, I can't **sleep** because of a terrible dream.'

I said: '**Sweet** woman, I **feel** very sorry for you, but how can I help?'

She answered: 'Take me to the river **queen**.'

I was shocked. 'The river **queen**?' I asked. 'Who is she? Where does she live?'

The old woman rubbed her tired **feet** and pointed to a place not far away. When she smiled, I saw she had no **teeth**. I invited her into my **jeep** and we drove to the river. At the river, the old woman got out and went into the ice-cold water, **deeper** and **deeper**. Soon there was no more old woman! Then a voice called me: 'Stephanus!' I ran into the water – it was **freezing**! 'Thank you, Stephanus,' the voice said again, but I could see no-one. Who was talking to me? Where was the old woman? Then, on the water, I saw two **geese** swimming towards me. They were **green geese**! One sang in a **deep** voice, the same voice as the old woman's. The other goose came up to me and touched my **cheek** with her wing. Was this the river **queen**? I watched as both **geese** flew up into the sky and I never saw them again."

After hearing the story, the students can write four or five sentences, using some of the words from the board and information from the story.

---

2 Picture match

a. Below are groups of three words where the vowel sounds are different but the consonant sounds the same. Match 20 of these words to the pictures in the grid. Write the words on the lines below the pictures. You might like to use your dictionary to help you.

cheek – chick – cheque	hell – hill – heel
fat – feet – fight	slip – sleep – slap
shop – ship – sheep	wheel – well – wall
teen – tin – ten	bite – beet – bat

13	14	15	16
....	....	....	....
17	18	19	20
....	....	....	....

b. Working in pairs, students take turns in making up sentences, each time using one of the words from the grid. Partners have to cross off the words as they are used, for example, I have two hands and two **feet**. (Cross off the word-picture of **feet** from the grid.) Do as many as possible within five minutes.

C Advanced

1 See the verbs

There are a number of single-syllable verbs that have 'ee' in the middle, for example, *keep*. Ask the students to think of more verbs that follow this spelling pattern and write them on the board. You could add to their list from the verbs below. The list might look like this:

breed bleed creep cheer feed feel freeze jeer keep
kneel meet need seek seem sleep speed sweep weed
weep wheel

Ask the students for the past tense of each verb and add these to the board. The board might now look like this:

breed – bred	bleed – bled	creep – crept
cheer – cheered	feed – fed	feel – felt
freeze – froze	jeer – jeered	keep – kept
kneel – knelt	meet – met	need – needed
seek – sought	seem – seemed	sleep – slept
speed – sped	sweep – swept	weed – weeded
weep – wept	wheel – wheeled	

Explain to the students that a close look at these past tenses will show that they can be divided into three main spelling patterns, with two verbs that are exceptions, or 'extras'. What are these patterns? Note students' suggestions. The answer to the question can easily be seen in the following grid:

ee → e	ee → e_t	+ed	'extras'

Ask the students to copy it into their notebooks, completing it with the correct verbs.

The full grid should look like this:

ee → e	ee → e_t	+ed	'extras'
breed – bred	creep – crept	cheer – cheered	freeze – froze
bleed – bled	feel – felt	jeer – jeered	seek – sought
feed – fed	keep – kept	need – needed	
meet – met	kneel – knelt	seem – seemed	
speed – sped	sleep – slept	weed – weeded	
	sweep – swept	wheel – wheeled	
	weep – wept		

Erase the board and have the students close their notebooks. Students can now do one of the following activities:

a. Ask students to recall the verbs in each group, for example, how many verbs do you remember that ended with 'e_t' in their past form?

b. While working in pairs, students make up 'silly sentences', using at least two of the verbs from the grid, in either the past or base forms, and one other 'ee' word, for example, I **felt** I should **sweep** the floor but instead I went to **Greece**.

---

2 Is a friend in need a friend indeed?

Choose an appropriate expression or phrase from the box below in order to complete the story logically.

knock her into the middle of next week   shoot the breeze

biting the hand that feeds you   black sheep

sweet as sugar   under my feet   wolf in sheep's clothing

keep my eyes peeled   count sheep   turn the other cheek

cheered up   green fingers   sneezed at

My brother George went to prison. He is the (1) .... of the family. So, while he was locked up, his girlfriend, Sarah, asked to move in with me. She showed her gratitude by stealing my wallet. That's (2) ....! George wrote to say I should forgive Sarah. You know – (3) .... But I was still feeling angry enough to (4) .... However, since I'm a good sister, I let Sarah stay, knowing that I would have to be very careful and (5) .... As the days went by, I realized that Sarah was really a (6) .... She pretended to be as (7) ...., but in fact she only (8) .... my hospitality. I only (9) .... when, one day, Sarah left. She was no longer (10) .... and I had some peace and quiet again.

Suggested words for spelling test

1 *Beginners*

green	teeth	cheek	feet	sleep
week	jeep	feel	queen	sweet

2 *Intermediate*
Some of these words have suffixes.

squeeze	bleed	freeze	sleeve	wheel
feed	meeting	weekly	sweeten	Greek
cheese	street	feelings	heel	speech

3 *Advanced*
Some of these words have suffixes.

between	breeding	sweetness	discreet	cheeky
seedling	cheerful	needless	fleeting	deepen
squeezed	sheepish	breezy	geese	wheeling

Answers

A1a

1 queen   2 teeth   3 sleep   4 feet   5 green   6 see   7 week
8 three   9 sheep   10 cheeks   11 wheels   12 tree

B2a

1 heel   2 shop   3 fat   4 cheek   5 ship   6 sleep   7 wheel   8 ten
9 slip   10 hill   11 well   12 chick   13 bite   14 fight   15 feet
16 hell   17 bat   18 wall   19 sheep   20 tin

C2

1 black sheep
2 biting the hand that feeds you
3 turn the other cheek
4 knock her into the middle of next week
5 keep my eyes peeled
6 wolf in sheep's clothing
7 sweet as sugar
8 sneezed at
9 cheered up
10 under my feet

8.2 'ea'

Lesson plan

In this lesson we are going to look at the spelling pattern 'ea', which is another common way of spelling the sound /iː/, as in *clean, dream*. This pattern mainly appears in the middle of words, but it is sometimes found at the beginning of a word, as in *easy* and *eat*. There are also a few words that end in 'ea' as in *tea* or *sea*.

Note:
Although the most common sound for the spelling pattern 'ea' is /iː/ as in *clean* it has four other sounds, which you may like to introduce, according to the level of your class. These sounds, in the order of their frequency, are:

/e/ in words such as *head, bread, thread, sweater, health, weather, heaven*.

/eɪ/ in words such as *steak, break, great, pear, wear, bear*.

/ɜː/ in words such as *early, earth, earn, learn, pearl, heard, search*.

/aː/ in *heart*.

1 INTRODUCTION: Write the following words on the board:

  read   dream   clean   team   please

  Read the words out loud and ask the class to compare them to 'ee' words learnt in the previous lesson, such as *green, need* and *cheese*.

2 REMIND students that there is no rule that tells us whether the sound /iː/ is spelled 'ee' or 'ea' when it is followed by a consonant sound.

3 ASK: What spelling pattern can we deduce from this? Note students' suggestions.

4 WRITE ON THE BOARD:

> Another common way of spelling the sound 'e' when it says its name in the middle of a one-syllable word is
>
> 'ea'.

You might like to write the following words which begin in 'ea' on the board:

each   ease   easy   eagle   ear   eat   eager   east

There are also a few words that end in 'ea':

sea   tea   pea

Suggest that students add this to their notebooks.

Warm-up practice of 'ea' spelling pattern

* *Beginners*
Write the following words, at random, on the board:

**red   ear   it   are   cheap   at   hear   read   her   rich
chip   reach   men   eat   mean   seat   man   sit**

Choose ten words to read out. Instruct the students to write down the words they think they hear.

* *Intermediate*
Using the same list of words, read out the words at random, without writing them first on the board, and ask the students to write down each word they hear. Remind students that all the words that have the sound /iː/ are spelled 'ea'.

* *Advanced*
Read out five of the following pairs of words at random and ask the students to write down each word they hear. Remind students that all the words that have the sound /iː/ are spelled 'ea':

**feast   fist   neat   net   leap   lip   heal   hill
peach   pitch   leak   lick   beard   bird   lease   less**

After reviewing the answers, you might want to suggest that the students write sentences of their own that include both words of the minimal pairs.

A Beginners

1 Solve and search

a. The answers to the clues are all words with 'ea'. Write the answer to each clue on the line. Do as many as you can. Compare your answers with a partner.

1 It comes from an animal and we eat it. ...*meat*...

2 We can start a letter like this: '........................... Mr Smith.'

3 Cold and sweet and good to eat! ....

4 Not hard or difficult. ....

5 To listen. ....

6 Not dirty. ....

7 To say something. ....

8 Something hot to drink. ....

9 Twelve months. ....

10 When you sleep you often ....

11 Not war. ....

12 We .... books and then we understand them.

13 Breakfast or lunch is a ....

14 The person who teaches you. ....

15 You have one on each side of your head. ....

16 Close, not far away. ....

17 When you ask for something, say: '........................... .'

18 What you do with your food: .... it.

19 Winter or summer, for example. ....

20 True, not false. ....

b. Now try to find each 'ea' word in the grid. Follow the example in the grid. Search from left to right and from top to bottom.

A	T	P	U	C	E	A	P	Q
D	V	E	P	L	E	A	S	E
R	E	A	D	R	M	J	C	A
E	S	C	I	M	E	A	L	R
A	P	E	A	O	E	N	E	A
M	E	A	T	K	D	E	A	R
B	A	S	E	A	S	O	N	E
D	K	L	A	W	H	A	A	R
I	C	E	C	R	E	A	M	E
E	A	T	H	E	A	R	Z	A
M	M	E	E	F	S	E	G	L
N	E	A	R	X	Y	E	A	R

© Cambridge University Press 2000

B Intermediate

1 What I mean is ...

As you read out each sentence, ask students to identify and write the 'ea' word that has been incorrectly used. Students should then write a suitable 'ea' word to replace it.

1 There was no more war after the two countries made **speak**.
(Students write down the word **speak,** and then the word **peace.**)

2 The sun always rises in the **beat**.

3 In the **teacher** of the summer, we often go down to swim in the pool.

4 Don't look at another student's test because it is **dreaming**.

5 'Have no **ice cream,**' said Superman. 'I am here to save you.'

6 In the autumn, the **beards** fall from the trees.

7 Please be **cleaned**. There are enough chairs for everyone.

8 I have two eyes, a nose, a mouth and two **peas**.

9 I feel so **real** today – I haven't had any food all day.

10 She opened her mouth and started to **steam** when she saw a mouse.

11 It is wrong to **repeat** something that is not yours.

12 **Seas** grow on trees and are a delicious fruit.

13 Don't **hear** your supper quickly or you will have a stomach-ache.

14 **Mean** John, I want to see you soon.

15 What are your **years** for choosing this car?

2 Neat meanings

Copy the following grid onto the board.

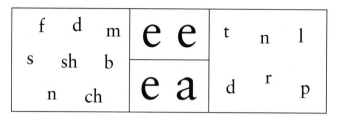

Students must find as many words as possible, where 'ea' or 'ee' will either be in the beginning, middle or end positions. Allow the students five minutes to complete this task, writing the words they find in their notebooks.

After completing this task, students could pair rhyming words together and try to form rhyming couplets.

C Advanced

1 Stop me, please!

a. Instruct the students that they will hear 30 words read out slowly. Most of the words are spelled with 'ea'. Students must call out 'Stop, please!' when they recognize a word that is spelled 'ee' and not 'ea'.

eat	reach	seal	least	teeth	peach	ideal	reason	green
leave	bleed	bead	feast	near	queen	heat	year	meal
speak	dream	cheer	clean	leaf	ear	easy	tree	cream
please	teacher	speed						

b. Read out the words again and then ask the students to work in pairs to recall as many words as possible. You might like to have each pair join with another pair to complete the list. One member from each group reports to the class.

2 Homonym pairs

There are a number of homonyms that have the same /iː/ sound, but are spelled either 'ee' or 'ea', for example, *flee – flea*. Choose appropriate words from the box to complete Mother's note below.

reed – read	Deer – Dear	seams – seems	leak – leek
bean – been	meat – meet	weak – week	see – sea
tee – tea	beech – beach	reel – real	steel – steal
team – teem	weak – week		

(1)........................ Alex

Dad won't be home. He's gone to the (2)........................ with Willy. (I think Willy will prefer to play on the (3)........................ . He has (4)........................ sick all (5)........................ .)

Sorry I'm not at home right now to (6)........................ you, but I have left you a few instructions. (7)........................ them very carefully, please!

a. There is a (8)........................ in the tap: try to fix it.

b. Take the (9)........................ out of the freezer.

c. We've run out of coffee, so you'll have to drink (10)........................ . Sorry!

d. Please pick up some (11)........................ nails at the store then finish building a proper bike stand so no-one will (12)........................ your bike again.

e. Oh, yes – your basketball captain phoned. Congratulations! You've made the (13)........................ ! It (14)........................ that you're a (15)........................ champion.

I'll be home in an hour or two.

Love,
Mum

Suggested words for spelling test

1 Beginners

meat	clean	easy	east	please
read	year	sea	eat	hear

2 Intermediate

fearful	appear	eastern	reason	cheating
each	beard	peaceful	teacher	feast
mean	screamed	beneath	dear	leaves

3 Advanced
This list includes 'ee' words.

cheer	disease	creature	teatime	disappearing
sweeten	wheeling	proceed	hearsay	weekday
agreement	ideally	greasing	breathe	underneath

Answers

A1a

1 meat   2 Dear   3 ice cream   4 easy   5 hear   6 clean   7 speak
8 tea   9 year   10 dream   11 peace   12 read   13 meal   14 teacher
15 ear   16 near   17 please   18 eat   19 season   20 real

A1b

A	T	P	U	C	E	A	P	Q
D	V	E	P	L	E	A	S	E
R	E	A	D	R	M	J	C	A
E	S	C	I	M	E	A	L	R
A	P	E	A	O	E	N	E	A
M	E	A	T	K	D	E	A	R
B	A	S	E	A	S	O	N	E
D	K	L	A	W	H	A	A	R
I	C	E	C	R	E	A	M	E
E	A	T	H	E	A	R	Z	A
M	M	E	E	F	S	E	G	L
N	E	A	R	X	Y	E	A	R

B1

1 peace   2 east   3 heat   4 cheating   5 fear   6 leaves   7 seated
8 ears   9 weak   10 scream   11 steal   12 peaches   13 eat
14 Dear   15 reasons

B2

Possible answers:
beet   beat   bean   bee   been   beer   beep   bead / cheat   cheer
cheap   cheep / dear   deer   deed   deep   deal   dean / eat   ear
eel / feet   feat   feel   fear   feed / meet   meat   meal / neat   near
need / sheet   sheep / sea   seat   see   seen   seed

C2

1 Dear   2 sea   3 beach   4 been   5 week   6 meet   7 Read
8 leak   9 meat   10 tea   11 steel   12 steal   13 team
14 seems   15 real

8.3 '-y'

Lesson plan

Note:
This lesson introduces the letter '-y' with the sound /iː/ at the end of a
word that has two or more syllables, as in *family* and *party*. There are
many words that follow this straightforward spelling pattern.

1 ELICIT: Ask students to suggest words that have the /iː/ sound in the
   end and have two or more syllables. Write the words on the board.
   Possible examples:

   happy   city   family   jelly

Common exceptions

If the following words are suggested, write them in a separate column
on the board because they are irregular and should be learnt globally:

degree   agree   pedigree   movie

You might want to point out to your students that two common '-y'
words – **granny** and **aunty** – are often spelled **grannie** and **auntie**.

There is a group of nouns that end in '-ey'. You could introduce them to your class as exceptions. The most common of these nouns are:

**monkey   donkey   turkey   money   honey   hockey   jockey
valley   alley   journey   chimney   storey   attorney**

2 ASK: What spelling pattern can we deduce from this? Note students' suggestions.

3 WRITE ON THE BOARD:

> When we hear 'e' saying its name at the end of a word
> that has two or more syllables, we write
> '-y'.

Adding a suffix

You might like to point out the following:

1 Plurals or third person singular in the Present Simple of words that end in consonant + '-y', change the 'y' to 'i' and add '-es', for example,

   carry – carries   family – families

2 When you need to add '-ed' (for the Simple Past) to words that end in consonant + 'y', change the 'y' to 'i' and add '-ed', for example,

   carry – carried   copy – copied

3 When you need to add '-er' or '-est' (for comparatives and superlatives of adjectives), change the 'y' to 'i' and add '-er' or '-est', for example,

   happy – happier – happiest

4 When you need to add '-ly' (for forming adverbs), change the 'y' to 'i' and add '-ly', for example,

   happy – happily   angry – angrily

Suggest that students copy this and the exceptions into their notebooks.

Because this spelling pattern is so straightforward, it is not necessary to reinforce it with a warm-up practice.

A Beginners

1 Categories

From the box, find two words for each category and write them in the grid. Then add two more words of your own to at least four categories. Note: 'Granny' and 'aunty' can also be spelled 'grannie' and 'auntie'.

biology	sleepy	thirty	Billy
snowy	sorry	cloudy	granny
eighty	Cathy	chemistry	aunty

Weather	Family	Numbers

Subjects at school	Feelings	Names

2 If you …

Complete the sentences with a suitable '-y' word. Do at least 11.

1 If you win some money, you will feel ....

2 If you break a plate, you may say, 'I'm ....'.

3 If you hear a joke, you will laugh if it's ....

4 If you go to an Indian restaurant, you can eat ....

5 If you are tired, it may be because you are ....

6 If you go to Scotland, you may see where they make

   ....

7 If you want to have fun with your friends, you can have a

   ....

8 If you take a holiday in Europe, you may visit ....

9 If you want to eat something sweet, you could have some

   ....

10 If you want to borrow a book, you can go to the

   ....

11 If you don't do any homework, the teacher may think

   you're ....

12 If you don't eat all day, you will feel ....

13 If you have a messy room, you may want to .... it.

14 If you love dogs, you may want to have a little ....

15 If you can't lift a big box, it may be very ....

B Intermediate

1 Scrambled adverbs

In order to find each adverb, read the sentence clue then unscramble the letters and add 'ly'. Write your answer in the space provided. Now copy each circled letter, in the order they appear, to the spaces below the grid. When completed, you will be able to read the famous proverb.

Clue	Letters	
1 How you might wait for a letter from a loved one.	e l f p u o h	+ ly =
	(h) o p e f u l l y	
2 How you go home if you're in a hurry.	i e t c r d	+ ly =
	_ _ _(_)_ _ _ _	
3 How you might walk if you failed a test.	d a s	+ ly =
	_(_)_ _ _	
4 How you might shout at a football game.	l o d u	+ ly =
	(_)_ _ _ _ _	
5 How you should work in a library.	l s n e t i	+ ly =
	_ _ _ _ _(_)_ _	
6 How a small child might run to his parents.	a p i p h	+ ly =
	(_)_ _ _ _ _ _	
7 How you walk after scoring a winning goal.	r u d p o	+ ly =
	_ _ _ _ _ _(_)	

The sound 'e' (/iː/)

8 How you might greet a friend.	r m w a ◯ _ _ _ _ _	+ ly =
9 How you should save money.	i s e w _ _ _ ◯ _ _	+ ly =
10 How you should play a game.	f r a i _ ◯ _ _ _ _	+ ly =
11 How a bee collects honey.	i s b u _ _ _ _ ◯ _	+ ly =
12 How you might smile for a photo.	e e w s t _ _ _ _ ◯ _ _	+ ly =
13 How ice cream slides down your throat.	s o o h t m _ _ _ _ _ ◯ _ _	+ ly =
14 How you should carry eggs.	e u l c r f a _ _ _ _ _ _ _ ◯	+ ly =

Early to bed and early to rise, makes a man _ _ _ _ _ _ _ ,

_ _ _ _ _ _ _ and wise.

222

2 Photo album

a. Use the correct forms of the words given above each picture to complete the sentences. Remember the spelling rule for changing 'y' to 'i' before adding certain suffixes, like 'ed', 'es'.

1 happy – angry

Dad is the .... one in the picture. Mum seems

.... than Dad, but neither of them is looking at me

very ....

2 marry – forty

My grandparents got .... in the nineteen

....

3 **lady – baby – easy**

The two .... holding the .... are my

aunts. They can .... carry ten more!

b. Draw two pictures to add to the photo album and write one or
two sentences for each. Include forms of words that belong to the
'-y' spelling pattern from this lesson.

C *Advanced*

1 *Cross-quotes*

a. Complete the crossword by deciding on the missing word from
each quotation or proverb. You can work with a friend and use
your dictionary.

Across

  4 Liberty, ... , fraternity! (French Revolution cry)
  5 .... is the country that has no history. (Proverbs)
 10 .... is the best policy. (Proverbs)
 13 Ali Baba And The .... Thieves. (Story title from *Arabian
     Nights*)
 14 .... had a little lamb. (Hale – Nursery Rhyme)
 15 .... is strength. (Proverbs)
 16 Trust not a new friend nor an old .... (Kelly)
 19 More the .... (Heywood)
 20 Land of hope and .... (Benson)
 21 Hush-a-bye ...., on the tree top. (Nursery Rhyme)

Down

1 As .... as an eel. (Proverbs)
2 .... hands make light work. (Proverbs)
3 I am .... when I am idle. (Ward)
6 A sound mind in a sound .... (Juvenal)
7 A land flowing with milk and .... (Bible)
8 In for a ...., in for a pound. (Proverbs)
9 .... days hath September. (Grafton)
11 .... is altogether in the eye of the beholder. (Hungerford)
12 An .... marches on its stomach. (Napoleon)
13 Do you believe in ....? (Barrie – from *Peter Pan*)
16 .... dog has his day. (Heywood)
17 The love of .... is the root of all evil. (Bible)
18 .... is bunk. (Henry Ford)

b. With the class, you can discuss the following:
- the meaning of the proverbs and quotations
- situations where you might use them
- translations in their mother tongue
- similar proverbs or sayings in their mother tongue
- which of the proverbs are still relevant today

c. You may like to give students the key words used in the answers to have them recall the full proverbs and quotations.

Suggested words for spelling test

1 *Beginners*

marry	happy	baby	lady	funny
windy	sleepy	daddy	Italy	lucky

2 *Intermediate*
This list includes suffixes.

tidier	silliest	money	babies	many
safety	rainier	happily	every	craziest
married	diary	holiest	studied	lazily

3 *Advanced*
This list includes suffixes as well as exceptions.

moodier	nasty	buried	guiltily	botany
Hungary	monkey	honey	sorrier	noisiest
loyalty	machinery	destiny	greedily	casualties

Answers

A1

Possible answers:
Weather: snowy, cloudy, windy, foggy, rainy, stormy, sunny
Family: granny, aunty, daddy, mummy, baby, nanny
Numbers: thirty, eighty, twenty, forty, fifty, etc.
Subjects at school: biology, chemistry, geography, history, anatomy, botany
Feelings: sleepy, sorry, angry, happy, funny
Names: Cathy, Billy, Teddy, Sally, Mary, etc.

A2

(Students may find different words.)
1 happy/lucky 2 sorry 3 funny 4 curry 5 sleepy 6 whisky
7 party 8 Germany/Italy/Hungary 9 jelly/candy 10 library
11 lazy 12 hungry 13 tidy 14 puppy 15 heavy

B1

1 hopefully 2 directly 3 sadly 4 loudly 5 silently 6 happily
7 proudly 8 warmly 9 wisely 10 fairly 11 busily 12 sweetly
13 smoothly 14 carefully

Early to bed and early to rise, makes a man healthy, wealthy and wise.

B2a

1 angriest, happier, happily
2 married, forties
3 ladies, babies, easily

C1a

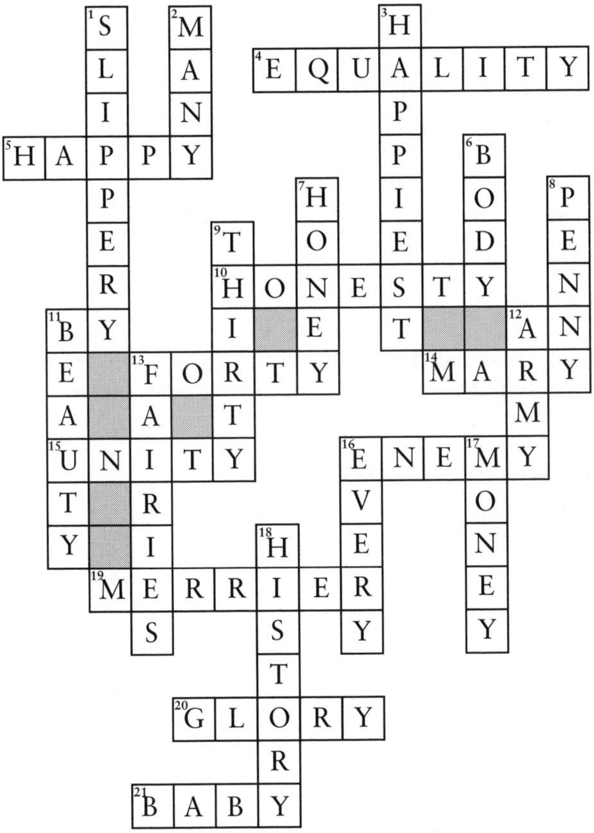
1 SLIPPERY
2 MANY
3 HAPPIEST
4 EQUALITY
5 HAPPY
6 BODY
7 HONEY
8 PENNY
9 THIRTY
10 HONESTY
11 BY
11 BEAUTY
12 AN
12 ARMY
13 FORTY
13 FAIRIES
14 MARY
15 UNITY
16 ENEMY
16 EVERY
17 MONEY
18 HISTORY
19 MERRIER
20 GLORY
21 BABY

8.4 'ie' and 'ei'

Lesson plan

Note:

1 These two spelling patterns are the third choice for spelling the sound /iː/ in the <u>middle</u> of a word, as in *receive, piece* and *fierce.* Applying the well-known spelling rhyme of 'I before E except after C' will help students most of the time. There are only a handful of words at the beginner's level, so we suggest you teach this pattern according to the needs of your students. The lesson plan and exercises in this lesson are aimed at the intermediate and advanced levels.

2 You may want to remind students that in Unit 5, the letters 'ei' were mentioned as an <u>irregular</u> spelling pattern for the sound /eɪ/ as in *reindeer, weigh, sleigh, eight, freight* and *neighbour.*

3 You might want to point out that in one-syllable words, the 'ie' at the end of a word is pronounced /aɪ/ as in *tie* and *pie.*

1 WRITE ON THE BOARD: Write the following 'ei' and 'ie' words on the board:

    piece   niece   chief   field   ceiling   receive

2 ASK: What are the two different spelling patterns that make the long 'e' sound /iː/ ?

3 ELICIT: Ask students to suggest other words with these spelling patterns.

Common exceptions

If the following words are suggested, write them in a separate column on the board since they do not follow the 'I before E except after C' rule and should be learnt globally:

    caffeine   codeine   protein   weird   seize

4 ASK: What spelling pattern can be deduced from this? Note students' suggestions.

5 WRITE ON THE BOARD:

> When we hear 'e' saying its name in the middle of a
> word our third choice will be to write
>
> 'ie'
>
> except if it follows 'c', and then we write
>
> 'ei'.

You might suggest that students add the spelling patterns and the relevant exceptions to their notebooks.

Warm-up practice of the 'ie'/'ei' spelling pattern

* Intermediate
The purpose of this listening exercise is to strengthen the visual-aural perception of the sound /iː/ spelled 'ie' as in *piece* as well as the sound /siː/ spelled 'cei', as in *receive*.

On the board write the following words, <u>omitting</u> the 'ie' and 'cei':

th**ie**f   pr**ie**st   c**ei**ling   n**ie**ce   bel**ie**ve   ch**ie**f
p**ie**ce   f**ie**rce   cash**ie**r   re**cei**ve

Instruct the students that as you read out the words they are to write the words in full into their notebooks, filling in the missing letters, 'ie' or 'cei'. Before you begin, you might like to remind them of the 'I before E except after C' rule.

* Advanced
The purpose of this listening exercise is to strengthen the visual-aural perception of the sound /iː/ spelled 'ie' as in *piece* as well as the sound /siː/ spelled 'cei', as in *receive*.

Have the students draw two columns in their notebooks, one headed 'IE' and the other 'EI'. As you call out the following words, instruct them to write each word in the appropriate column. You might want to remind them of the rule: 'I before E except after C'.

deceive   achievement   relief   shield   receipt   shrieked   pierce
misconceive   thieves   priesthood   disbelieve   conceited   briefly
chandelier   retrievable

A Intermediate

1 'What am I ?'

Write the following words on the board:

> protein   niece   ceiling   believe   priest   caffeine
> receive   thief   achieve   chief   chandelier

You might like to begin by first pointing out that 'protein' and 'caffeine' do not follow the 'I before E except after C' rule.

Instruct the students to draw four columns in their notebooks with the following headings: People, Food, Home, Verb. Have them copy the words from the board into the column with the most suitable heading. Quickly review their answers.

Now, read out a definition for each word, but in random order. You should begin, 'My first definition is ...' or, 'Number one is ...'. Students write the number of the definition beside the appropriate word.

Return to the words on the board, and erase the 'ie/ei' in every word. (You could erase some or all words from the board if your class's level supports this.) Allow the students to study the words in their notebooks for half a minute before putting them away. Call out a definition. A correct answer will consist of identifying both the correct word and whether it is spelled 'ie' or 'ei'.

2 Mix and complete

In order to find the answer to the clue in column 1, mix up the letters of the short word in column 2 and place them into the spaces of the word in column 3. Do as many as you can.

1	2	3
1 Shortly; concisely.	L I B	_ R _ E F _ Y
2 Form of defence.	L I D S	_ H _ E _ _
3 Faith.	F I B	_ E L _ E _
4 Very aggressive or angry.	I C E	F _ E R _ _ _
5 The top of a room.	L E G	C _ I _ I N _
6 Not one (together with 'nor').	H I R E	N _ _ T _ E _

© Cambridge University Press 2000

7 People who steal.	V E T S	__ H I __ __ E __
8 Small parts.	S I P	__ __ E C E __
9 The person you pay in a shop, maybe.	R A C E	__ __ S H I __ __
10 Your brother's daughters.	S I N	__ __ E C E __
11 Meadows, areas of open land.	S I D E	F __ __ L __ __ __
12 A man of the church.	T I P	__ R __ E S __

B Advanced

1 A piece of advice

Work with a partner, taking turns to ask five questions each. Each answer should include a word that has 'ie' or 'ei'.

1 When you want to pay for your groceries in the supermarket you go to the ...

2 In a luxurious home, instead of a simple light fixture you may want a ...

3 The answer to 2 could be hung from the ...

4 In order to look fashionable, you might want to get your ears ...

5 Some people do this when they see a mouse. They ...

6 Where would you find a place to dock a yacht? At a ...

7 Your room needs decorating so you paint a scene on a long strip of paper and put it high up on the wall. You have just made a ...

8 Don't drink too much coffee because it has ...

9 You are on a special diet to build up your body. Milk, eggs, and meat are important because they have lots of ...

10 You need to find the plural for the noun 'thief' in order to start your story: *Ali Baba and the Forty* ...

© Cambridge University Press 2000

2 Pair crossword

In this activity you will work with a partner and complete a crossword. Work together, but do not look at your partner's puzzle. You and your partner will be completing the same crossword, but each of you has different information. Therefore, before you begin, write down a suitable clue or hint for the words you have on your page, for example, *lion – a wild animal, a big cat*.

When you have both finished writing down your clues, take turns asking for information that each of you needs to complete your crossword puzzle. If necessary, you may give more than one clue. All the words in the puzzle follow the spelling patterns you have learnt in this unit.

Student A

Across

7 underneath ....

8 dreams ....

15 yearly ....

16 believe ....

17 niece ....

18 flea ....

Down

1 freedom ....

2 clean ....

3 seized ....

9 key ....

10 receive ....

13 holy ....

Student A

FREEDOM
CLEAN
SEIZED
UNDERNEATH
DREAMS
YEARLY
BELIEVE
HOLY
RECEIVE
NIECE
FLEA

Student B

Across

2 city ....

4 fierce ....

6 cozy ....

12 either ....

19 peace ....

Down

5 many ....

6 cheese ....

7 uneasy ....

8 deep ....

11 brief ....

14 reel ....

Suggested word list for spelling test

1 *Intermediate*

ceiling	thief	receive	relieve	chief
niece	cashier	weird	fierce	believe
seize	priest	thieves	piece	deceive

2 *Advanced*

protein	disbelieve	deceitful	piercing	chieftain
retrieval	seized	misconceive	shriek	receipt
pier	grieving	perceive	aggrieved	received

Answers

A2

1 briefly   2 shield   3 belief   4 fierce   5 ceiling   6 neither
7 thieves   8 pieces   9 cashier   10 nieces   11 fields   12 priest

B1

An alternative is to read the situations to the class, who write answers individually.

1 cashier   2 chandelier   3 ceiling   4 pierced   5 shriek   6 pier
7 frieze   8 caffeine   9 protein   10 Thieves

B2

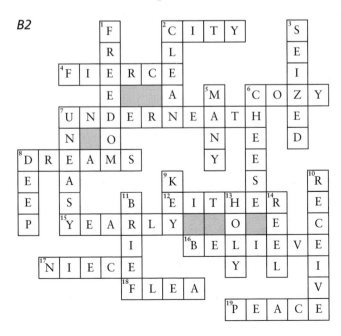

9 Soft and hard sounds (/s/, /g/ and /dʒ/)

9.1 The soft 'c'

Lesson plan

This unit deals with two letters that have both 'hard' and 'soft' sounds: 'c' and 'g'. The soft 'c' and 'g' occur when they are followed by the letters 'i', 'e' and 'y', as in *pencil, cell, fancy, giant, angel* and *gym*.

This lesson studies the sound /s/ when it is spelled with the letter 'c'. Although the most frequent spelling patterns for the /s/ sound are 's' and 'ss' (as in *sit* and *miss*), there are many words where 'c' is used instead. It is called the **soft** 'c' in order to differentiate it from the **hard** 'c' which has the sound /k/, as in *cat*. You may like to review quickly the lesson on the use of 'c' or 'k' in Unit 2, as well as the lesson on short vowel followers, which included '-ss', in Unit 3.

Note:
Unfortunately, there is no 'rule' to help students decide whether to write 's' or 'c' when they hear the /s/ sound, but a growing awareness of soft 'c' words should help improve their spelling. A few spelling generalizations are described below. Teach them according to the needs of your class.

- The letter combination 'ce' is more common than 'ci' and 'cy'. It usually appears in the middle or end of a word, and is considered irregular when it begins a word as it does in *cell, centre, ceremony* and *certain*.
- We often find '-ence' or '-ance' as the final syllable in multi-syllable words, such as *audience* and *appearance*.
- Many adjectives that end in '-ant' and '-ent' have a noun-form that ends in '-ance' or '-ence', as in *silent–silence* and *ignorant–ignorance*.
- It might be worth pointing out to your more advanced students that there is sometimes a difference between British and American spelling. British spelling prefers '-ence', while the American spelling will sometimes be '-ense', as in *defence* (Br.) and *defense* (Am.). Another difference can be seen with the word 'practice'. American

spelling does not differentiate between the spelling of *practice* when used as a verb or a noun, while British spelling does differentiate between the two, writing *practice* (n.) and *practise* (v.).

- When we hear /s/ at the end of a single-syllable word, we usually write 'ce', if:
  1 it is preceded by a long vowel sound (as in *place* and *mice*)
  2 it is preceded by the letter 'n' or 'r' (as in *France* and *fierce*)
- When we hear the sound 'see' (/sɪ/) at the end of a multi-syllable word, we usually write 'cy' as in *fancy*, *democracy* and *secrecy*.

1 WRITE ON THE BOARD:

   fence   cat   clown   cent   crazy   Lucy   coke   pencil   pick

2 ASK: What letters follow the soft 'c'? On the board, draw three columns and write the headings: **cy ci ce**

3 ELICIT: Ask students to suggest other 'cy', 'ci' and 'ce' words, and add them to the grid. Alternatively, you could ask the students to scan a textbook page or article to find three words for each category.

Common exceptions

If the following words are suggested, you may want to write them in a separate column, since they are spelling or pronunciation exceptions:

scene   scent   science   scissors   ascend   descend   chase base   case   rinse   sense   tense

4 ASK: What spelling patterns can we deduce from this? Note students' suggestions.

5 WRITE ON THE BOARD:

> 1 We sometimes write 'c' when we hear the sound 's' before the letters 'i', 'e' and 'y'.
>
> 2 We usually write 'ce' when we hear the sound 's' at the end of a one-syllable word in the singular.
>
> 3 We usually write 'cy' at the end of a multi-syllable word when we hear the sound 'see'.

Suggest that the students copy this and the exceptions into their notebooks.

Adding a suffix

You might like to remind your students of the following:
When adding a suffix that does *not* begin with an 'i' (like '-ing') to words which end in consonant + 'y', you first change 'y' to 'i' before adding the suffix, for example,

city + s = cities   fancy + ed = fancied

BUT fancy + ing = fancying

Warm-up practice of 'ce', 'ci' and 'cy' spelling pattern

* *Beginners*
The purpose of this listening exercise is to strengthen the audio-visual awareness of the soft and hard 'c'. Draw the following grid on the board and ask the students to copy it into their notebooks, numbering the rows one to ten downwards:

	Soft 'c'	Hard 'c'
1		

Write the following words on the board:

can   city   pencil   crazy   prince   face   corn   Nancy
Cyprus   clock

Ask the students to say the words silently to themselves and write them in the appropriate column.

* *Intermediate*
The purpose of this listening exercise is to strengthen the audio-visual awareness of the soft 'c' when it is pronounced /s/ as in *cell*. Explain to the class that for this exercise, when they hear the /s/ sound followed by 'e' or 'i', the preceding letter will be 'c'. An /s/ sound followed by all other letters will be 's'. Included also are one-syllable words in the singular that end in 'ce'.

Ask the students to write the numbers 1–15 in a column in their notebooks. As the teacher reads the following pairs of words, students try to identify the 'c' word, writing '1' if it is the first word and '2', if it is the second. For more able students, you might suggest they write the 'c' word.

salt – ceiling   cement – slow   nice – pants   citizen – steal
grass – space   officer – mister   past – decide   ask – Nancy
bats – price   cinema – store   receive – fast   eats – ice
mystery – excite   medicine – listen   disaster – bicycle

* *Advanced*
The purpose of this listening exercise is to strengthen the audio-visual
awareness of the soft 'c'. Follow the instructions for the intermediate
exercise, but have students write out both words.

A Beginners

---

1 Twice is nice

Read through the four-lined verses, then choose rhyming words
from the box to complete each one. There are three extra words.
Do as many as you can.

peace	police	chance	race	ice
twice	France	face	nice	Greece
niece	price	dance	mice	place

1 It's very ....
   To drink juice with ....
   When the sun is hot
   You can drink a lot.

2 I must make ....
   With my little ....
   We had a fight –
   It wasn't right.

3 If you get lost in ....
   You can ask the ....
   Then come with us
   To Mount Olympus.

4 What is the ....
   Of two white ....?
   I hope it's not a lot.
   A pound is all I've got.

5 Who got first ....
   In the running ....?
   It was not fun
   Because I can't run!

6 If you like to ....
   Then come to ....
   But there isn't samba
   Or even mamba!

---

2 Island fun

Read each clue and write the answer, one letter in each box. Now write the corresponding letter in the same number box below to discover the names of two beautiful Mediterranean islands.

1 New York is a very big ☐ ☐ ☐ ☐(11)

2 A king and queen live in a ☐ ☐(12) ☐(5) ☐ ☐ ☐

3 One mouse, two ☐ ☐ ☐(3) ☐

4 A place to see clowns ☐ ☐ ☐ ☐ ☐(14) ☐

5 Your brother's daughter is your ☐(8) ☐ ☐ ☐(10) ☐

6 This is cold and good to eat – ☐(2) ☐ ☐ cream

7 The king's daughter is a ☐ ☐(13) ☐ ☐ ☐ ☐(15) ☐

8 It has two wheels and it's fun to ride – a ☐ ☐(4) ☐ ☐(6) ☐ ☐ ☐

9 Some men smoke this – a ☐ ☐ ☐ ☐(7) ☐

10 Waltz and tango are ☐(9) ☐ ☐ ☐ ☐(1)

1	2	3	4	5	6	7	8	9	10	11	12	13	14	15
☐	☐	☐	☐	☐	☐	☐	☐	☐	☐	☐	☐	☐	☐	☐

B Intermediate

1 The 'c' code

a. Choose ten phrases from the left-hand list below and write them on the board. Explain to the students that each phrase is a sound-alike for a soft 'c' word, for example, **sell her = cellar**. Working in pairs, students write down their answers. Allow four or five minutes before eliciting and writing the students' answers on the board.

Phrase	Soft 'c' word
sit tea	city
grow, sir	grocer
saw sir	saucer
sit is Zen	citizen
sir call	circle
can sell	cancel
sir tan	certain
add all less sent	adolescent
sent you ray	century
sigh ants	science
at ten dance	attendance
prints 's'	princess
I scream	ice cream
off is her	officer

b. In pairs, students try to create more 'sound-alike' phrases for soft 'c' words. Possible words are *pencil*, *dancing*, *celery* and *centre*.

Soft and hard sounds

---

2 Syllabox

In order to work out the answer to each clue, you need to select one syllable from each of the boxes. Each answer will be a three-syllable word. Write your answer on the line beside the clue. Do as many as you can.

1 Not guilty. *innocent*

2 A two-wheeled vehicle. ....

3 Round. ....

4 Moving forward. ....

5 The work of a genius, maybe. ....

6 Drug to treat disease. ....

7 Person who fights crime. ....

8 Very, very good. ....

9 Foodstuff. ....

10 A hundred years. ....

11 Place to see a movie. ....

12 One who studies biology, maybe. ....

po bi	cer ter	ing ~~cent~~ ies
sci mas	cel i en	cine cle
gro ad cin	~~no~~ vanc cy	man piece lar
~~in~~ cir	cu e	ma lent
med cen ex	lice tu	ry tist

© Cambridge University Press 2000

242

C Advanced

1 Nounsearch

a. Below is a list of adjectives that end in '-ent' or '-ant'. By changing these endings to '-ence' or '-ance' they become nouns, for example, *innocent–innocence*. Search up and down and from left to right to find at least ten nouns in the grid.

absent   resistant   intelligent   significant   confident
silent   different   ignorant   present   excellent
violent   important   patient

I	M	P	O	R	T	A	N	C	E	S	C	I
B	V	R	S	N	P	X	A	V	X	I	L	N
S	I	L	E	N	C	E	C	I	C	G	C	T
P	O	C	C	O	N	F	I	D	E	N	C	E
A	L	A	B	S	E	N	C	E	L	I	N	L
T	E	C	C	E	N	F	L	N	L	F	C	L
I	N	C	E	N	C	T	Y	C	E	I	B	I
E	C	V	I	G	N	O	R	A	N	C	E	G
N	E	R	Z	E	C	U	A	I	C	A	X	E
C	P	R	E	S	E	N	C	E	E	N	C	N
E	C	D	I	F	F	E	R	E	N	C	E	C
R	E	S	I	S	T	A	N	C	E	E	C	E

© Cambridge University Press 2000

b. Use some of the nouns you found to complete these sentences. You may want to use a dictionary to help. Do as many as you can.

1 The police do not like the rise in ....

2 Scientists have discovered that dolphins are clever animals, with high ....

3 We often see a sign with the word '.........................' in a library, telling us not to speak.

4 The .... of driving carefully should be taught in school.

5 We should aim for .... in whatever we do.

6 Diving from a cliff requires skill and a lot of ....

7 Do you know what the .... is between a Siamese and a Persian cat? I do!

8 Some people say that '......................... is bliss', instead of saying, 'What you don't know can't hurt you'.

9 Your rude behaviour is trying my ....

10 You weren't in school yesterday. The teacher noted your

....

2 Crossword-story

In order to complete the crossword, read the following story. The missing words in the story are the answers to the crossword. All the missing words follow either the 'ce' or 'ci' spelling pattern. Fill in as many words as you can.

The Royal Lesson

(*1. Down*) upon a time, not so very long ago, the king and queen of (*6. Across*) lived in the (*20. Down*) of Paris. They were very happy ... (*14. Across*) for the fact that their son, Henri, loved to (*11. Down*). It didn't matter what kind – it could be the twist, samba, waltz or tango. Just give him a room with lots of (*22. Across*), a girl with a pretty (*23. Across*), some good music, and off he went, dancing until morning. Unfortunately, sometimes this got him into trouble!

Well, late one night, there was a knock at the door of the royal (*8. Across*). It woke up the king, who went to the door to see what was the matter.

'I'm sorry to disturb you,' the man said. 'I'm Inspector Marcel, from the Paris (*16. Down*). I am afraid that I have to speak to you about your son.'

'Oh, dear,' said the king, 'What has Henri done now?'

'I've just come from the movie at the local (*15. Down*),' said the Inspector. 'It seems that while Henri was dancing he got into a fight. I had to arrest him for disturbing the (*13. Down*).'

'Hmm,' said the king. 'Where is my son now?'

'He's in a (*2. Down*), down at the police station,' replied the Inspector.

'Thank you, (*1. Across*),' the king said. 'I'll come and get him out.'

Several hours later, the king and Henri were in court. Henri was holding a bag of (*7. Across*) over a bump on his head and looking very sorry for himself.

'Young man,' the judge said in a serious (*12. Across*), 'you have no (*21. Across*) but to begin to behave like a royal (*8. Down*). You will do 50 hours of community (*9. Down*) to pay for your bad behaviour.'

'Yes, sir,' said Henri. 'I am really sorry for what I did.'

The king and his son went home without saying a word. Finally, the king spoke up. 'I know what you need, you need a good woman. I am going to talk to my cousin, Alphonso. He lives in Athens, the capital of (*19. Across*). His brother's daughter, Alphonso's (*17. Down*), is just the right woman for you. *And*, she is a (*3. Down*) too!! She's the daughter of good King Milos. I am going to ask him to (*10. Across*) you to her. She is a very (*18. Down*) young woman. I am (*5. Down*) she will be a good (*4. Down*) on you – and that is just what you need, my son!'

Suggested words for spelling tests

1 *Beginners*
These words follow the 'ce', 'ci', and 'cy' spelling patterns.

dance	Greece	Lucy	pencil	ice
bicycle	cinema	juice	princess	city

2 *Intermediate*
These words include the 'ce', 'ci', and 'cy' spelling patterns.
Some words have suffixes/prefixes.

choice	citizens	exercising	recently	forceful
society	circle	replace	Cyprus	attendance
icy	excellent	circle	cancel	century

3 *Advanced*
These words include the 'ce', 'ci', and 'cy' spelling patterns and a
few common exceptions. Some words have suffixes/prefixes.

saucy	descendant	citrus	incidentally	censor
scenery	infancy	cylinder	deception	sincerely
capacity	decipher	innocent	cynical	etcetera

Answers

A1

1 nice, ice   2 peace, niece   3 Greece, police   4 price, mice
5 place, race   6 dance, France

A2

1 city   2 palace   3 mice   4 circus   5 niece   6 ice   7 princess
8 bicycle   9 cigar   10 dances

The words in the boxes are: Sicily and Cyprus.

B2

1 innocent   2 bicycle   3 circular   4 advancing   5 masterpiece
6 medicine   7 policeman   8 excellent   9 groceries   10 century
11 cinema   12 scientist

C1a

I	M	P	O	R	T	A	N	C	E	S	C	I
B	V	R	S	N	P	X	A	V	X	I	L	N
S	I	L	E	N	C	E	C	I	C	G	C	T
P	O	C	C	O	N	F	I	D	E	N	C	E
A	L	A	B	S	E	N	C	E	L	I	N	L
T	E	C	C	E	N	F	L	N	L	F	C	L
I	N	C	E	N	C	T	Y	C	E	I	B	I
E	C	V	I	G	N	O	R	A	N	C	E	G
N	E	R	Z	E	C	U	A	I	C	A	X	E
C	P	R	E	S	E	N	C	E	E	N	C	N
E	C	D	I	F	F	E	R	E	N	C	E	C
R	E	S	I	S	T	A	N	C	E	E	C	E

C1b

1 violence   2 intelligence   3 silence   4 importance
5 excellence   6 confidence   7 difference   8 Ignorance
9 patience   10 absence

248

C2

```
 ¹O  F  F  I  ²C  E  R          ³P     ⁴I     ⁵C
  N           E            ⁶F  R  A  N  C  E
 ⁷I  C  E     L                 I     F     R
  E     ⁸P  A  L  A  C  E        N     L     T
 ⁹S     R                       C     U     A
  E  ¹⁰I  N  T  R  O ¹¹D  U  C  E     E     I
  R     N                 A     S     N     N
¹²V  O  I  C  E           N     S     C
  I     E       ¹³P       C     E
  C           ¹⁴E  X ¹⁵C  E ¹⁶P  T
  E     ¹⁷N     A     I     O           ¹⁸N
  I        I     C     N     L           I
¹⁹G  R  E  E  C  E     E     I        ²⁰C  C
  C        C     M  ²¹C  H  O  I  C  E
²²S  P  A  C  E     ²³F  A  C  E        T
                                       Y
```

9.2 The soft and hard 'g'

Lesson plan

In this lesson we look at two sounds of 'g': the soft 'g', pronounced /dʒ/ as in *gentle*, and the hard 'g' pronounced /g/ as in *good*. Generally, when the letter 'g' is followed by 'e', 'i', or 'y', it is pronounced as a soft 'g', as in *gentle*, *magic* and *gym*. (This is similar to the lesson on the soft 'c', so you may like to point this out to your students.) Alternatively, when 'g' is followed by 'a', 'o', 'u', 'l' or 'r', it is pronounced as a hard 'g', as in *game*, *go*, *gun*, *glad* and *grow*.

Note:
There are many common words (often at the beginner's level) that do not follow this rule, for example, *get*, *give* and *girl*. Many of these 'exceptions' are words that do not originate directly from the Latin.

A few spelling generalizations are described below. Teach them according to the needs of your class.

- When we hear /dʒ/ at the end of a single-syllable word, preceded by a short vowel sound, we usually write '-dge', as in *fudge*. (You may like to remind your students of '-dge', one of the short vowel followers in Unit 3.)

- When we hear /dʒ/ at the end of a word preceded by a long vowel sound or a consonant, write '-ge' as in *page* and *barge*. English words never end in 'j'.
- If we hear the sound /g/ followed by 'e' or 'i', we often write 'gu', as in *guess* or *guilty*. A rare form is 'gh', as in *ghost* and *ghastly*.

1 WRITE ON THE BOARD: Write the following words on the board and have the students say them quietly to themselves:

age   giant   apology   guess   wagon   gallon   great

2 ASK: What letters follow the 'g' when it is 'soft'? On the board, draw three columns and write the headings:

gy   gi   ge

3 ELICIT: Ask students to suggest other 'gy', 'gi' and 'ge' words, and add them to the grid.

Common exceptions

If the following words are suggested, you may want to write them in a separate column, since they are pronunciation exceptions where 'g' has a hard sound:

begin   bogey   get   geyser   gift   giggle   gimmick   girl girdle   give   finger   forget   forgive   hunger   guarantee tiger   together

4 ASK: What spelling patterns can we deduce from this? Note students' suggestions.

5 WRITE ON THE BOARD:

> 1 We usually write 'g' when we hear the sound 'j' before the letters 'i', 'e' and 'y'.
> 2 We write '-ge' when we hear the sound 'j' at the end of a word.
> 3 When we hear the sound 'g' before 'i' or 'e', we often write 'gu'.

Suggest that the students copy this and the exceptions into their notebooks.

Warm-up practice of the soft and hard 'g' spelling patterns

The purpose of this listening exercise is to strengthen the audio-visual awareness of the soft and hard 'g'.

* *Beginners*
Draw the following grid on the board and ask the students to copy it into their notebooks, numbering the rows one to ten downwards:

	Soft 'g'	Hard 'g'
1		

Write the following words on the board:

> orange   go   giant   Germany   dogs   guess   golf   large
> giraffe   angry

Ask the students to say the words quietly to themselves and write them in the appropriate column.

* *Intermediate*
Write the following words on the board, omitting the letters that are emphasized, replacing each of these letters with a short line, for example, __ __ m (gym). Say each word twice, slowly. Students write down the full word.

> gym   garage   energy   garbage   teenager   guest   giant
> engineer   geography   dangerous   bridge   guest   stranger
> guitar   language

* *Advanced*
Using the word list from the previous intermediate exercise, call out each word for the students to write down in their notebooks.

A Beginners

1 Soft 'G' signs and notices

a. For each sign or notice, complete the sentence by choosing a suitable word from the box below.

1

2

3

4

5

6

giraffes   orange   LUGGAGE
pages   CHANGE   DANGER

b. Discuss with the students where they might find such notices.
c. Suggest that each student create a notice of his/her own using a soft 'g' word. You may want to make a class exhibition of the students' work.

2 What am I?

Note:
You may first want to review the spelling generalizations for the soft and hard 'g' as well as exceptions for this level. On the board, write the following words:

> get   Germany   geography   girl   goal   large   begin   angry
> forget   magic   finger   orange   together   giraffe   vegetable
> page   golf   big   George   change   hungry   Argentina   tiger

Divide the class into two teams. Each team chooses a name for itself that includes the letter 'g'. Write the team names on the board. As the teacher *silently* points to a word at random in the list, teams take turns to identify the word as **soft 'g'**, **hard 'g'** or **irregular**. Keep score by putting a tick under the appropriate team's name. When a team answers incorrectly, the second team is allowed to answer as a bonus point, before continuing on to their turn.

When all the words have been reviewed, you may want to repeat words that were difficult for the class to identify correctly. Now, remove the words from the board, and allow the teams to compete by writing down as many words as they remember. The winning team has the most accurately spelled words that were on the original list.

B Intermediate

---

1 Geography quiz

How good are you at geography? Test your skills here! All the place names include the letters 'ge', 'gi' or 'gu' and they have been entered into the answer spaces to help you. You may want to look at a world map or atlas. Do as many as you can.

1 A country in West Africa. Its capital is Lagos.

   _ _ G E _ _ _

2 French and Flemish are spoken in this European country.

   _ _ _ G I _ _

---

3 This is a city in Morocco. _ _ _ G I _ _ _ _

4 A very big European country. G E _ _ _ _ _ _

5 A city in Holland. The _ _ G U _

6 A lake and city in Switzerland. G E _ _ _ _ _

7 This is one of the Channel Islands. G U _ _ _ _ _ _ _

8 This is a country in South America. _ _ G E _ _ _ _ _ _

9 The largest river in India. _ _ _ G E _

10 The capital city of the Czech Republic. _ _ _ G U _

11 A rock island in the Mediterranean. G I _ _ _ _ _ _ _ _

12 This country is in North West Africa. _ _ G E _ _ _ _

13 This region is in the north of South America. G U _ _ _ _ _

14 Both a state in the US and in Eastern Europe.
    G E _ _ G I _

15 Both a group of islands and part of the Mediterranean Sea.
    _ _ G E _ _

---

2 Scrambled Gs

Work in pairs to unscramble the mixed-up word to complete the meaning of the sentence. Write the word on the line provided. Do as many as you can.

1 A person is innocent, until proven **yuiglt.** ....

2 'Who's the boss, here?' 'Mike is in **rhecag.**' ....

3 'You drive me bananas!' is a **refuig** of speech. ....

4 He collects **getsopa** stamps. ....

5 My shoes are made of **nugieen** leather. ....

6 The tour **digeu** showed us the old streets of Paris.

....

7 People say that the world is now a global **gellaiv**.

....

8 Jules Verne wrote a wonderful book entitled *20,000 gueeaLs Under The Sea.* ....

9 The secret service has many special **tegnas**, like James Bond 007. ....

10 Come on in and be my **estug**! ....

11 'Mr Speaker, ladies and **lengmeent**, good evening.'

....

12 Sell your old furniture at a **raggae** sale. ....

13 George is going to Brazil on a student **gancheex** programme this summer. ....

© Cambridge University Press 2000

C Advanced

1 Mind game

Ask students to think silently of a word that contains 'g'. The first student calls out the first letter of his/her 'g' word, without revealing what the word is. For example, s/he might be thinking about the word 'anger', so the first letter would be 'a'. The next student in turn must now think of a 'g' word which begins with 'a'. Possibly, the second student might also think of 'anger' so would reply 'n'. On the other hand, the second student might think of another word, such as 'agree', so the reply would be 'g'. The next student must now add a third letter to the word. If the class feels any answer is based on an incorrect guess, they may challenge the answer. Students who cannot justify their answers by supplying the word, or students who fail to answer, drop out of the game until the next word. Once a 'g' word has been spelled completely, ask for the first letter of a new word.

In later rounds you might want to increase the difficulty. An additional challenge would be that students must avoid completing a word, even if it is the first syllable of a longer word. Those who complete a word also drop out of the game.

---

2 Scrambled quotations

a. Unscramble the letters to form a logical word to complete each famous quotation. Write the word you form on the line. Do as many as you can.

1 **onigReil** .... is the opium of the masses. (Karl Marx)

2 All the world's a **gaets** ....
And all the men and women merely players.
(William Shakespeare)

3 So God created man in his own **megai.** .... (Bible)

4 ... love and **raiegram** .... rarely can combine. (Byron)

5 One should never trust a woman who tells her real **eag.**

.... (Oscar Wilde)

6 **nuisGe** .... is one per cent inspiration and ninety-nine per cent perspiration. (Thomas Edison)

7 To err is human, to **vgfeior** .... divine.
(Alexander Pope)

8 It is better that ten **yigtlu** .... men escape than one innocent suffer. (Sir William Blackstone)

9 Fools rush in where **gnalse** .... fear to tread.
(Alexander Pope)

10 **eagInim** .... there's no heaven,
It's easy if you try. (John Lennon)

---

11 The **geswa** .... of sin are death. (Bible)

12 It's as **galre** .... as life and twice as natural!
(Lewis Carroll)

b. If you wish, you can choose the quotations most meaningful, or useful, to you. In pairs, or as a class, explain your choices.

© Cambridge University Press 2000

Suggested words for spelling tests

1 *Beginners*
The following words include the soft 'g' and the irregular, hard 'g' words of this level.

change	girl	Germany	magic	give
age	large	get	orange	begin

2 *Intermediate*
These words include the soft 'g', hard 'g' and irregular words for this level.

giant	hunger	energy	religion	guest
argue	danger	agent	teenager	guitar
finger	manager	language	figure	stranger

3 *Advanced*
These words include the soft 'g' and hard 'gu', as well as irregular words for this level. Some words have a prefix or suffix.

courageous	digestion	guilty	lodgings	register
enlarge	genesis	giggle	argument	vaguely
forgiven	apologetic	geometry	guardian	prestige

Answers

A1a

1 luggage   2 orange   3 giraffes   4 danger   5 change   6 pages

B1

1 Nigeria   2 Belgium   3 Tangiers   4 Germany   5 The Hague
6 Geneva   7 Guernsey   8 Argentina   9 Ganges   10 Prague
11 Gibraltar   12 Algeria   13 Guyana   14 Georgia   15 Aegean

B2

1 guilty   2 charge   3 figure   4 postage   5 genuine   6 guide
7 village   8 Leagues   9 agents   10 guest   11 gentlemen
12 garage   13 exchange

C2a

1 Religion   2 stage   3 image   4 marriage   5 age   6 Genius
7 forgive   8 guilty   9 angels   10 Imagine   11 wages
12 large

10   Odds and ends

10.1 Silent letters

Lesson plan

In this unit we look at three sources of spelling errors: silent letters; the sound /ʃən/ when it is the final syllable '-tion' and '-sion'; and the sound /əl/, spelled '-le', '-al' and '-el', heard at the end of words with two or more syllables.

This lesson introduces the most common of the silent letters. They are 'silent partners' in a consonant pair, and can come before or after the voiced consonant. In the following examples, the silent letter is emphasized: *wr – write, kn – knife, gn – sign* and *lk – walk*. (For a more complete list, see the Elicit exercise below.)

Some of these letters, like the 'k' in *knife* and the 'g' in *gnaw*, used to be pronounced several hundred years ago, and were introduced by the Vikings ('kn') and the Anglo-Saxons ('gn').

Unfortunately, there are no 'rules' to help us identify the silent letters. They are reading and writing patterns that have to be learnt through practice. For this reason, the warm-up listening exercises have been omitted.

1   WRITE ON THE BOARD: Write the following column headings. For beginners, you may want to omit patterns that are unfamiliar or infrequent at this level.

Example word	Silent letter	Silent letter + talking partner	More examples
know			
talk			
half			
palm			
why			

rhino			
comb			
sign			
would			
write			
listen			

2 ASK: What letter is silent, in each word? Write the students' answers in the appropriate column.

3 EXPLAIN: Refer to the column 'silent letter + talking partner', and explain that each silent letter has a 'partner' which 'does all the talking'. Ask students to find the 'talking partner' for each silent letter. Write both the silent letter and 'talking partner' in this column.

4 ELICIT: Ask students to suggest one or two more words for each silent letter, and write them in the last column.

Acceptable answers:

Example word	Silent letter	Silent letter + talking partner	More examples
know	k	kn	knife, knock, knot
talk	l	lk	walk, chalk, stalk
half	l	lf*	calf
palm	l	lm	calm, qualms, balmy
why	h	wh	where, when, why
rhino	h	rh	rhyme, rhythm
comb	b	mb	thumb, climb, bomb
sign	g	gn	foreign, reign, design
would	l	ld	could, should
write	w	wr	wrong, wrestle, wrap
listen	t	st	whistle, castle

*note '-lf' in plural: calf-calves

You might add the following for more advanced students:
'ch' (*stomach, archaeology, Christmas*)
'gh' (*ghost, gherkin, ghastly*)
'ps' (*psychiatry, psalms, pseudo-*)
'bt' (*doubt, subtle, debt*)

5 WRITE ON THE BOARD:

> Some words have consonant pairs,
>
> where one letter is silent
>
> **kn lk lf ld lm**
>
> **wh rh wr mb gn st**

Suggest that the students copy this and the examples into their notebooks.

A Beginners

1 Picture mix

In order to find the word in each box, use the picture and the scrambled letters to help you. Write the word on the line provided. Do as many as you can.

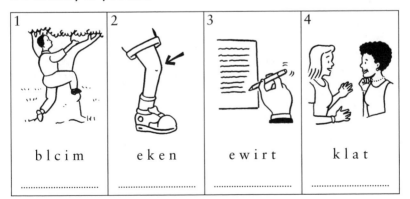

1	2	3	4
b l c i m	e k e n	e w i r t	k l a t
....	....	....	....

Odds and ends

5 e w h l e	**6** f e k i n	**7** s e i t l n	**8** k l w a
9 This is a stop- g i s n	**10** l f h a	**11** o h n r i	**12** k o k c n
13 m b u t h	**14** e l h w a	**15** s l e t c a	**16** m o b c

2 Categories trio

Listed below are 16 two-word categories. From the box, choose a suitable 'silent-letter word' to make them into three-word categories. Do as many as you can.

1 ankle, foot, ...

2 pencil, pen, ...

3 toe, finger, ...

4 think, hope, ...

5 dolphin, shark, ...

6 ball, circle, ...

7 red, yellow, ...

8 why, where, ...

9 brandy, vodka, ...

10 shout, speak, ...

11 spoon, fork, ...

12 puppy, kitten, ...

13 draw, print, ...

14 hippo, elephant, ...

15 empty, quarter, ...

16 run, jump, ...

wheel	rhino	write	know	walk	whisky
	chalk	when	knee	talk	knife
	thumb	white	half	lamb	whale

Now give a name to describe each category. Do as many as you can.

B Intermediate

1 Silent search

a. Hidden in the grid are words with silent letters. How many can you find of the following?

- six words with the silent letters 'kn'
- four words with the silent letters 'wh'
- three words with the silent letters 'wr'
- three words with the silent letters 'mb'
- three words with the silent letters 'rh'
- three words with the silent letters 'gn'
- three words with the silent letters 'lk'

K	N	O	W	L	E	D	G	E	D	U	M	B
Y	B	R	H	Y	M	E	S	E	W	I	N	C
J	C	K	I	G	C	K	W	R	H	I	N	O
W	H	I	S	K	Y	N	A	F	E	W	W	M
L	A	X	T	N	D	O	L	K	E	R	R	B
A	L	V	L	I	T	T	K	N	L	O	E	W
M	K	X	E	F	O	R	E	I	G	N	S	R
B	E	Y	U	E	I	Z	J	G	U	G	T	I
W	H	I	S	P	E	R	V	H	G	N	L	S
N	S	I	G	N	R	H	Y	T	H	M	E	T
T	E	D	E	S	I	G	N	K	N	O	C	K
T	A	L	K	T	U	K	N	E	E	K	F	K

b. Write a word from the grid that matches each definition. Do as many as you can.

1   A drink that Scotland is famous for. ....

2   Coming from abroad; not from your own country.

    ....

3   A very large, rare African animal. ....

4   It's sharp and used for cutting. ....

5   To talk in a very low voice. ....

6   To make a loud noise through your teeth. ....

7   Sir Lancelot was one. ....

8   A young sheep. ....

9   Material used to write on a blackboard. ....

10 Not right. ....

11 You might use it to make your hair tidy. ....

12 To write your name, at the end of a letter maybe.

    ....

C *Advanced*

1 Sentence fill

By reading each sentence and using the letter clues, you can find the missing words. Do as many as you can.

1   The king is our _ _ _ _ _ _ _ _ g ʌ and has

    _ _ _ g ʌ _ _ for many years.

2   I don't have enough strength in my k ʌ _ _ _ _ _ _ _ in

    order to k ʌ _ _ _ this bread dough.

3 The _ _ c h _ _ _ _ _ _ played and the c h _ _ _ _ sang at the opening of the new opera.

4 Arms and legs are _ _ m b _ and you have eight fingers and two _ _ _ m b _ on each hand.

5 I always feel quite sad and _ _ _ _ m n when summer turns into _ _ _ _ m n.

6 I read a scary g h _ _ _ _ story about evil spirits and g h _ _ _ _ _ .

7 Sir Lancelot was a brave k n _ _ _ _ _ and he k n _ _ how to use his sword very well.

8 Stan has a _ _ _ _ _ _ c h _ c h _ : he must have eaten too much.

9 Can you tell me w h _ _ _ _ _ _ a w h _ _ _ _ is a fish or an animal?

10 W r _ _ _ _ _ _ _ _ is a dangerous sport: you might break your arm or sprain your w r _ _ _ .

---

2 Do you know?

Do you know a 'silent letter' word that answers each question? Do as many as you can.

Do you know ...

1 ... a 'gn' word meaning a biting insect? ....

2 ... a 'ch' word meaning a plan? ....

3 ... a 'gh' word meaning a kind of cucumber? ....

4 ... a 'kn' word meaning a sharp cutting tool? ....

5 ... an 'mb' word meaning a burial chamber? ....

6 ... a 'wh' word meaning a type of grain used to make bread?...........................

7 ... an 'lf' word meaning a young cow? ....

8 ... a 'bt' word meaning a sum of money that is owed?

....

9 ... a 'wr' word meaning anger? ....

10 ... an 'rh' word meaning musical tempo or beat? ....

11 ... an 'lk' word meaning to speak? ....

12 ... a 'ps' word meaning a song of praise? ....

13 ... an 'ld' word meaning ought to? ....

14 ... an 'mn' word meaning a long section on a printed page?

....

15 ... an 'lm' word meaning peaceful? ....

Suggested words for spelling test

1 *Beginners*

white	know	half	wrong	walk
knife	talk	listen	write	thumb

2 *Intermediate*

rhino	could	design	palm	kneel
comb	where	castle	calf	wrist
chalk	knowledge	wheel	knock	foreign

3 *Advanced*

resign	wretched	subtle	archives	scheme
wheat	plumber	solemnly	orchestra	doubtful
psychiatry	womb	calf	ghastly	Christmas

Answers

A1

1 climb   2 knee   3 write   4 talk   5 wheel   6 knife   7 listen
8 walk   9 sign   10 half   11 rhino   12 knock   13 thumb
14 whale   15 castle   16 comb

A2

1 knee   2 chalk   3 thumb   4 know   5 whale   6 wheel   7 white
8 when   9 whisky   10 talk   11 knife   12 lamb   13 write
14 rhino   15 half   16 walk

B1a

K	N	O	W	L	E	D	G	E	D	U	M	B
Y	B	R	H	Y	M	E	S	E	W	I	N	C
J	C	K	I	G	C	K	W	R	H	I	N	O
W	H	I	S	K	Y	N	A	F	E	W	W	M
L	A	X	T	N	D	O	L	K	E	R	R	B
A	L	V	L	I	T	T	K	N	L	O	E	W
M	K	X	E	F	O	R	E	I	G	N	S	R
B	E	Y	U	E	I	Z	J	G	U	G	T	I
W	H	I	S	P	E	R	V	H	G	N	L	S
N	S	I	G	N	R	H	Y	T	H	M	E	T
T	E	D	E	S	I	G	N	K	N	O	C	K
T	A	L	K	T	U	K	N	E	E	K	F	K

'kn' words: knight, knife, knock, knot, knowledge, knee
'wh' words: whisky, wheel, whisper, whistle
'wr' words: wrist, wrong, wrestle
'mb' words: dumb, comb, lamb
'rh' words: rhino, rhyme, rhythm
'gn' words: sign, foreign, design
'lk' words: chalk, walk, talk

B1b

1 whisky   2 foreign   3 rhino   4 knife   5 whisper   6 whistle
7 knight   8 lamb   9 chalk   10 wrong   11 comb   12 sign

C1

1 sovereign, reigned   2 knuckles, knead   3 orchestra, choir
4 limbs, thumbs   5 solemn, autumn   6 ghost, ghouls
7 knight, knew   8 stomach, ache   9 whether, whale
10 Wrestling, wrist

C2

1 gnat   2 scheme   3 gherkin   4 knife   5 tomb   6 wheat   7 calf
8 debt   9 wrath   10 rhythm   11 talk   12 psalm   13 should
14 column   15 calm

10.2 '-tion' and '-sion'

Lesson plan

This lesson introduces the two most common ways for spelling the
sound /ʃən/: '-tion' as in *station* and '-sion' as in *tension*. These
patterns are often the final syllable in words of two or more syllables.
This includes many verbs made into nouns by simply dropping the
final 'e', or changing the end of the root word before adding the
suffix '-tion', as in *appreciate – appreciation* or '-sion', as in
admit – admission.

We also include the final syllable '-sion' when pronounced /ʒən/, as
in *conclusion*. For further details about this pronunciation, see below.

Since there are few beginner words with these two spelling patterns,
the lesson plan and exercises are at the intermediate and advanced
levels.

Note:
You may want to point out to your students a few common
generalizations for '-tion' and '-sion'. Teach them according to the
needs of your class:

• The most common spelling pattern for the sound /ʃən/, is '-tion',
  followed by '-sion'.

- There are two distinct sounds for '-sion'. The first, /ʃən/ as in *tension*, has the same sound found in words spelled with '-tion'. Students may be helped by knowing that many words spelled with '-sion' are preceded by 's', 'l', 'r' or 'n', as in *mission, convulsion, version* and *pension*.
  The second sound for '-sion' is /ʒən/, as in *conclusion*. Words that end with this sound are generally spelled '-sion', with the common exception of *equation*.
- A third spelling pattern is '-cian', as in *physician*, added to words that end in '-ic'. The new word, derived from the original '-ic' word, usually describes a person who works in that particular field, for example, *magic – magician* and *mathematics – mathematician*.
- Far less common for the sound /ʃən/ are the following spelling patterns: '-tian' (*Egyptian, Martian*); '-sian' (*Russian, Asian*); and '-shion' (*cushion, fashion*).

1 WRITE ON THE BOARD: Draw a large, inverted triangle, and label it as shown:

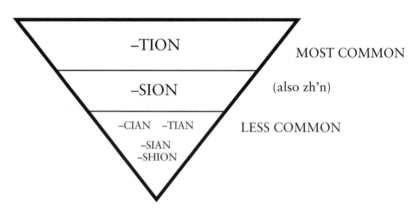

2 ELICIT: Ask students to suggest words of two or more syllables that end with the sound /ʃən/ and write them beside the appropriate section of the triangle. Possible answers:

'**-tion**': attention, conversation, addition, nation
'**-sion**': profession, tension, passion, expression
'**-cian**': musician, politician, physician
'**-tian**': Egyptian, Venetian, Martian
'**-sian**': Russian
'**-shion**': cushion

Ask students to suggest words that end with the sound /ʒən/ and write them in a different column, near the '-sion' section. Possible answers:

'**-sion**': conclusion, decision, occasion, invasion

Common exceptions

If words are suggested that end in '-tian', '-sian' and '-shion', you may want to write them separately, because they are exceptions, as are *suspicion* and *ocean*.

3 ASK: What spelling patterns can we deduce from this? Note students' suggestions.

4 WRITE ON THE BOARD:

> 1 When we hear the sound 'sh'n' at the end of a word with two or more syllables, our first choice is '-tion'.
>
> 2 When we hear the sound 'zh'n' at the end of a word with two or more syllables, our first choice is '-sion'.

Suggest that the students copy this and the exceptions into their notebooks.

Warm-up practice of the '-tion' and '-sion' spelling patterns

* Intermediate

The purpose of this listening exercise is to strengthen the auditory-visual awareness of the sound /ʃən/ spelled only as '-tion' for this exercise, and the sound /ʒən/ spelled '-sion'. On the board, write the following words, omitting the final syllable '-tion' or '-sion':

televi<u>sion</u> correc<u>tion</u> confu<u>sion</u> invita<u>tion</u> na<u>tion</u> vaca<u>tion</u> explo<u>sion</u> correc<u>tion</u> fic<u>tion</u> emo<u>tion</u> conclu<u>sion</u> educa<u>tion</u> sta<u>tion</u> ac<u>tion</u> deci<u>sion</u>

Read out each word in full; students write the whole word in their notebooks. Alternatively, you may first want to let the students try to write down the words in full, then let them self-check their answers when you read them out.

* Advanced

The purpose of this listening exercise is to strengthen the auditory-visual awareness of the sound /ʃən/ spelled '-tion' and '-sion'. Also included is the sound /ʒən/ spelled '-sion'. Write the following words on the board:

> addition pollution condition motion caution ambition
> regulation position comprehension permission profession
> collision occasion explosion confusion

Instruct the students to study the words for about 30 seconds. Erase the words. Explain that you will read out the words at random. Students write the words in their notebooks.

A Intermediate

---

1 Flower power

a. Find the answers to the clues by mixing up the letters in each petal and adding the letters '-tion' from the centre of the flower. Write the complete word on the line near each clue. Do as many as you can.

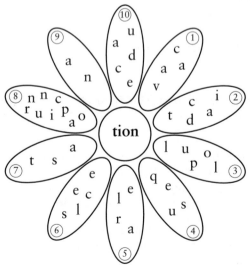

---

1 A holiday. ....

2 A spelling test, maybe. ....

3 Dirt in the air or water, maybe. ....

4 Something you ask. ....

5 Uncle or cousin. ....

6 A choice of things. ....

7 Place to catch a train. ....

8 The way we speak. ....

9 A country. ....

10 What you are receiving at school. ....

b. Now try to complete these sentences with some of the words from the flower.

1 Many people are very worried about the amount of

   .... there is in the world today. We must all work together to fight it!

2 The United ....s has its centre in a very large building in New York City.

3 I am so tired after all this work, I feel that I need a nice,

   long ....

4 I want to ask you a .... : how old are you?

5 If our .... is not clear, then others will have difficulty understanding what we are saying.

6 We have no choice – we must get a good .... to help us get a good job in the future.

7 Teacher told us that we have to learn the new spelling pattern

   for a .... tomorrow. I hope I get a good grade!

8 Can you tell me the way to the .... please? I have to meet my mother off the four o'clock train.

2 Mission possible

a. Write the following verbs on the board, checking to see that students understand their meaning:

**admit   conclude   confess   confuse   comprehend   decide
discuss   divide   express   explode   permit   invade**

Ask students to form '-sion' nouns from the verbs. They will have to make other changes to the word as well, which they can check in a dictionary. Allow five to ten minutes, depending upon the class level.

b. Invite students to see if they can find spelling generalizations for converting the verbs into nouns. Answers can include:

'-ude' → '-usion'; '-ade' → '-asion'; '-ide' → '-ision'; '-ode' → '-osion'

c. Suggest the students do one of the following activities listed below, using at least eight of the words from exercise a. Students should work individually, then pass their work to a partner to solve, read or comment upon.

1 Make up a crossword puzzle, with clues.
2 Make up a trivia quiz.
3 Make up a wordsearch with the base words as clues.
4 Make up a story.
5 Draw illustrations.

B Advanced

1 Complete the quotations

a. Choose one of the three words that correctly completes each quotation. Do as many as you can.

1 Truth is stranger than **conversation, fiction, admission.** (19th century proverb)

2 Was it a **reaction, decision, vision** or a waking dream? (Keats)

3 **Provision, Possession, Communication** is nine points of the law. (Draxe)

4 **Actions, Selections, Populations** speak louder than words. (20th century proverb)

5 Give me that man
  That is not **passion's, education's, conclusion's** slave.
  (Shakespeare)

6 Pride goes before **devotion, division, destruction** and a
  haughty spirit before a fall. (Proverbs, 16, 18)

7 Necessity is the mother of **invention, precision, adoption**.
  (16th century proverb)

8 **Education, Consideration, Action** begins a gentleman,
  conversation completes him. (Fuller)

9 **Omission, Passion, Confession** is good for the soul. (Kelly)

10 'Tis safest in matrimony to begin with a little **mission,
   aversion, conversation**. (Sheridan)

11 The better part of valour is **discretion, submission, regulation**.
   (Shakespeare)

12 In my Father's house there are many **mansions, selections,
   temptations**. (St John, 14, 2)

b. You may want to discuss some of these quotations, and how
important they are today. You can also categorize them, or rank
them according to personal preference.

© Cambridge University Press 2000

2 What's in a word?

a. On the board, write the word: C O N G R A T U L A T I O N S!
Explain to the class there are more than 20 words that end with
'-tion', '-tions' or '-tional' hidden in this word. Working in pairs,
they should find at least ten. After five to eight minutes, you might
encourage each pair to join with another pair to compare and
lengthen their lists. Each group of four students now competes with
the other groups for the longest and most correct list.

b. Have the students give a '-tion' name to their group. Write these
names on the board. Each group takes turns to call out a '-tion' word
from their list. They must be prepared to use it correctly in a sentence.
Groups cannot repeat a word suggested previously. Write each correct
answer under the appropriate group's name. The winning group is the
one with the longest list.

Suggested words for spelling test

1 *Intermediate*
The following words include the '-tion' and '-sion' spelling patterns.
Some words have the suffix '-s' or '-al'.

conditional	fiction	conclusion	vacation	station
television	decisions	instruction	national	explosions
correction	explanation	composition	dictation	invitation

2 *Advanced*
The following words include the '-tion' and '-sion' spelling patterns,
as well as the less common '-cian' made from '-ic' words. Some
words have suffixes.

population	station	occasionally	reaction	superstitions
optician	collision	passionately	ambition	electrician
reaction	dictionary	fictional	physician	air-conditioner

Answers

A1a

1 vacation   2 dictation   3 pollution   4 question   5 relation
6 selection   7 station   8 pronunciation   9 nation   10 education

A1b

1 pollution   2 Nation   3 vacation   4 question   5 pronunciation
6 education   7 dictation   8 station

A2a

admission   conclusion   confession   confusion   comprehension
decision   discussion   division   expression   explosion   permission

B1a

1 fiction   2 vision   3 Possession   4 Actions   5 passion's
6 destruction   7 invention   8 Education   9 Confession
10 aversion   11 discretion   12 mansions

B2a

This is what we found; there may be more:

congratulation   strangulation   translocation   granulation/s
transaction   coagulation   translation   carnation/s   salutation
saturation   location/s   notation/s   solution   traction/s/al
rotation/s   suction   auction/s   notion/s/al   sanction   caution/s
station   ration/s   action/s   nation/s/al

10.3 '-le', '-al' and '-el'

Lesson plan

This lesson covers the sound /əl/, when it is spelled '-le', '-al' or '-el' at the end of words with two or more syllables, such as *table*, *logical* and *rebel*. You may want to review quickly with your students the lesson on '-ll', in Unit 3.

Note:
Because '-le', '-al' and '-el' have the same sound in spoken English, students might benefit from a few spelling generalizations. However, be prepared for 'exceptions'. The more common generalizations are listed below. Teach them according to the needs of your class.

- Most nouns and verbs (with two or more syllables) ending with the sound /əl/ are spelled '-le', as in *table*, *cycle* and *apple*.
- Most words that end in '-al' are adjectives, as in *musical*, *usual*, and *general*. There are several common nouns which are exceptions, such as *sandal*, *animal* and *festival*.
- Common suffixes that include the sound /əl/ are: '-ible' as in *possible* and '-able' as in *washable*.
- Words that end in '-el' are fewer in number, and may have to be learnt globally. Most of the words are nouns and verbs, such as *towel* and *quarrel*.

1 WRITE ON THE BOARD:
Note:
Because there are few words at the beginner's level which end in '-el' and '-al', we suggest you limit the lesson to the '-le' ending. Instead of introducing the spelling pattern with the inverted triangle, illustrated below, we suggest you put up the letters '-le' on the board and elicit words for this spelling pattern. Possible words include:

little   jungle   table   uncle   middle

If words with '-el' or '-al' endings are suggested, write them in a separate column, to be learnt globally.

For intermediate and advanced levels, draw a large, inverted triangle and label it as shown:

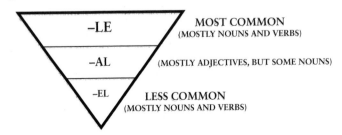

277

2 ELICIT: Ask students to suggest words of two or more syllables that end with the sound /əl/ ('-le', '-al', or '-el'), and write them in the appropriate section of the triangle.

Possible answers:
'-le': ankle, apple, bible, bottle, kettle, table
'-al': final, medical, normal, total, animal
'-el': camel, quarrel, parcel, travel, angel

3 ASK: What spelling patterns can we deduce from this? Note students' suggestions.

4 WRITE ON THE BOARD:

When we hear the sound 'l' at the end of a word with two or more syllables:

1 our first choice for a word which is a noun or verb is to write '-le'

2 our first choice for a word which is an adjective is to write '-al'

3 some words end in '-el'.

Suggest that the students copy this into their notebooks.

Warm-up practice of the '-le', '-al' and '-el' spelling patterns

* *Beginners*

The purpose of this listening exercise is to strengthen the auditory-visual awareness of the sound /əl/ by comparing words with two or more syllables that end with '-le' to single syllable words that end with '-ll'. Have the students copy the following table of ten rows into their notebooks.

-le	-ll

As you read out the following words, students must check off the appropriate column. More able students may want to write the words out in full.

**table   wall   bell   uncle   puzzle   jungle   kill   poodle
call   middle**

* *Intermediate*
The purpose of this listening exercise is to strengthen the auditory-visual awareness of two of the new spelling patterns for the sound /əl/: '-le' and '-al'. On the board, scatter the following words *without* the '-le' or '-al' endings:

**final   title   jungle   logical   battle   people   ankle   normal
middle   article   trouble   musical   triangle   able   practical**

Explain that for this listening exercise, when a word is a noun or verb, students must add '-le' to the beginning letters. Adjectives will end in '-al'. (You might want to review how we identify these parts of speech.) Point to the partially written word, then say the whole word. Students must identify the word as an adjective, noun or verb before adding the correct endings, and writing the whole word in their notebooks.

* *Advanced*
The purpose of this listening exercise is to strengthen the auditory-visual awareness of the two new spelling patterns for the sound /əl/: '-le' and '-al'. Explain that for this listening exercise, when a word is a noun or verb, students must add '-le' to the beginning letters. Adjectives will end in '-al'. Use the word list from the intermediate exercise. Call out each word slowly, for the students to write in their notebooks.

A Beginners

1 Word bubbles

a. Unscramble the letters in each bubble to form an '-le' word. Write the word on the line in the bubble.

1 n u l j g e _____

2 c e n l u _____

3 b a l e t _____

4 l t t i e _____

5 e o t b l t _____

6 l c n a d e _____

7 t t u l e r _____

8 p i l s m e _____

9 l t t i l e _____

10 e b i b l _____

11 p a l p e _____

12 z u p e l z _____

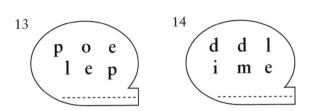

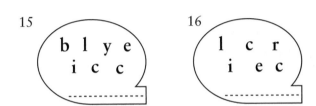

b. Match some of the words to their definitions. Do as many as you can.

1 A holy book.   ....

2 Men, women and children.   ....

3 Jigsaw or crossword.   ....

4 Your mother's brother.   ....

5 A tortoise in the sea.   ....

6 Not the beginning or end.   ....

7 Name (of a book, maybe).   ....

8 Red or green and good to eat.   ....

9 A forest in Africa, maybe.   ....

10 Easy, not hard.   ....

B *Intermediate*

1 *Definition sound-alikes*

In each box, find the two rhyming words by looking at the
definition and the rhyming end sound. Write the missing letters in
the space provided, then write out each word in full. Do as many
as you can.

	Definition	Missing letters	End sound	Write word
1	Kind of pasta		OODLE	
2	Kind of dog			
3	Four legs, flat top		ABLE	
4	Short story with moral			
5	A fight between armies		ATTLE	
6	Many cows together			
7	Two		OUBLE	
8	Difficulty	(2 letters)		
9	Burns on birthday cake		ANDLE	
10	Hold this, not the cup			
11	Salty/sour cucumber		ICKLE	
12	This makes you laugh			
13	Not high, not low		IDDLE	
14	Like a puzzle			

	Definition	Missing letters	End sound	Write word
15	You put it on a horse		ADDLE	
16	You use it in a kayak			

17	Very easy		IMPLE	
18	A red spot on the face			

19	Electric; boils water		ETTLE	
20	To get comfortable			

2 Which ending?

Read each clue, to help you identify the word. Decide whether it ends with '-le', '-el' or '-al'. A dictionary might be useful. Answer at least ten.

-LE?	-EL?	-AL?

1 The shape of an egg. O V __ __

2 A grey or red furry animal that eats nuts. S Q U I R R __ __

3 To cross out. C A N C __ __

4 You need this to sew. N E E D __ __

5 You can do this by boat, plane or car. T R A V __ __

6 The bone that joins your foot to your leg. A N K __ __

7 A shape with three sides. T R I A N G __ __

8 An argument. Q U A R R __ __

9 Doctors and nurses work there.   H O S P I T __ __

10 A big celebration, like in Rio de Janeiro. C A R N I V __ __

11 Exactly the same.   I D E N T I C __ __

12 An open shoe, often worn in summer.   S A N D __ __

13 A dog house.   K E N N __ __

14 A path or road under the ground.   T U N N __ __

15 A glass container.   B O T T __ __

C Advanced

1 Riddle scramble

Unscramble the letters by each definition to form an '-ible' or an '-able' word and write it on the spaces near the definition. Now write the letter that corresponds to each number on the spaces below. If you do it correctly, you will find the answer to our riddle!

Something that ...

1 ... is hard to remember is R B O E F G A L T T E

__ __ __ __ __ __ __ __ __ __ __
2   11

2 ... is very scary is R L H R I O B E

__ __ __ __ __ __ __ __
  7

3 ... you can understand is L E E G I T L L I I N B

__ __ __ __ __ __ __ __ __ __ __ __
      6

4 ... is sad and poor is E S E A M I R B L

__ __ __ __ __ __ __ __
        12

5 ... can be allowed is E P R I L E M I S S B

— —̲ — — — — —̲ — —
   15   4

6 ... cannot be seen is I V L E I S I B N

— — — —̲ — — — —
        10

7 ... is very cute is D B A O A R L E

—̲ — — — —̲ — — —
9   1

8 ... is really bad is L E E T R I B R

— — — — — —̲ —
          5

9 ... can be read is G E L E I B L

—̲ — — —̲ — —
14   13

10 ... may not succeed is I L B A F L L E

—̲ —̲ — — — — —
8 3

Riddle:
What do you think the story of the Fifth Labour of Hercules might
be called?

—̲   —̲ —̲ —̲ —̲   —̲ —̲   —̲   —̲ —̲ —̲ —̲ —̲ —̲!
1   2 3 4 5 6   7 8   9   10 11 12 13 14 15

2 Word match

a. Choose a word from box C that completes a phrase with a word in column A. Write this word in column B. The first one has been done for you. There may be more than one answer for some of the words.

A First word	B Noun from the box
1 official	whistle
2 ritual	
3 international	
4 tropical	
5 oval	
6 local	
7 formal	
8 fictional	
9 pedal	
10 intellectual	
11 mortal	
12 royal	

C

novel   rivals   table   title

puzzle   bicycle   proposal   burial

jungle   hospital   scandal   whistle

b. Listed below are examples where you might use one of the adjectival phrases from the previous exercise. This time, write the whole phrase on the line provided. Try to do it from memory.

1 A crossword puzzle could be this

....

2 *The Old Man And The Sea*

....

3 'Would you marry me, my fairest one?'

....

4 Her Majesty, the Queen

....

5 The pyramids are an example

....

6 A two-wheeled vehicle without motor

....

7 The Amazon area

....

8 It's blown at football games

....

9 The American President writes on one

....

10 Possibly, angry cats and dogs together

....

© Cambridge University Press 2000

Odds and ends

Suggested words for spelling tests

1 *Beginners*
   The following words include both the '-le' and '-ll' spelling patterns.

   ball   candle   well   apple   uncle
   bottle   puzzle   little   ankle   shell

2 *Intermediate*
   The following words include '-al' adjectives and '-le' nouns.

   trouble   final   candle   plural   poodle
   circle   people   capital   handle   rifle
   title   comical   needle   kettle   logical

3 *Advanced*
   The following words include the '-le', '-al' and '-el' spelling
   patterns. Affixes have been added to some words.

   miserable   gambler   expel   cable   external
   riddle   rebel   fable   impossible   impractical
   settled   cruelly   trembling traveller   typically

Answers

A1a

1 jungle   2 uncle   3 table   4 title   5 bottle   6 candle   7 turtle
8 simple   9 little   10 bible   11 apple   12 puzzle   13 people
14 middle   15 bicycle   16 circle

A1b

1 bible   2 people   3 puzzle   4 uncle   5 turtle   6 middle
7 title   8 apple   9 jungle   10 simple

B1

1 noodle   2 poodle   3 table   4 fable   5 battle   6 cattle   7 double
8 trouble   9 candle   10 handle   11 pickle   12 tickle   13 middle
14 riddle   15 saddle   16 paddle   17 simple   18 pimple   19 kettle
20 settle

B2

Note:
You may want to do this as a board activity. Draw the box and three
endings high enough on the board to enable you to write the partially
written answers below. Read each clue to the class, allowing students
to write down their answers in their notebooks. Alternatively, you
might want to ask volunteers to come up to write the answers on the
board.

1 oval   2 squirrel   3 cancel   4 needle   5 travel   6 ankle
7 triangle   8 quarrel   9 hospital   10 carnival   11 identical
12 sandal   13 kennel   14 tunnel   15 bottle

C1

1 forgettable   2 horrible   3 intelligible   4 miserable   5 permissible
6 invisible   7 adorable   8 terrible   9 legible   10 fallible
The riddle is: A fable of a stable.

C2a (Possible answers)

1 official whistle   2 ritual burial   3 international scandal
4 tropical jungle   5 oval table   6 local hospital   7 formal proposal
8 fictional novel   9 pedal bicycle   10 intellectual puzzle
11 mortal rivals   12 royal title

C2b

1 intellectual puzzle   2 fictional novel   3 formal proposal
4 royal title   5 ritual burial   6 pedal bicycle   7 tropical jungle
8 official whistle   9 oval table   10 mortal rivals

Recommended resources

Hickey, K., *Dyslexia: A Language Training Course for Teachers and Learners*, London: Kathleen Hickey Publications, 1977.

Pei, M., *The Story of English*, Greenwich: Fawcett Publications, Inc., 1965.

Scott, Foresman & Co., (eds), *Spelling Research and Information – An Overview of Current Research and Practices*, Illinois: ScottForesman, 1995.

Vellutino, Frank R., 'Dyslexia', *Scientific American* (March, 1987), Vol. 256, No. 3, 20–27.

Index

In this index, 'Lesson plans' and 'Warm-up (listening) practices' are in *italics*, the names of the activities are in **heavy type**, with the levels marked as follows:

B = Beginners
I = Intermediate
A = Advanced